FUNNY BUSINESS

FUNNY BUSINESS

HUMOUR, MANAGEMENT AND BUSINESS CULTURE

Jean-Louis Barsoux

CASSELL

Cassell
Villiers House, 41/47 Strand
London WC2N 5JE

387 Park Avenue South
New York, NY 10016-8810

First published 1993

British Library Cataloguing-in-Publication Data
A catalogue entry for this book is
available from the British Library.

ISBN 0-304-32677-1 (hardback)
    0-304-32821-9 (paperback)

Typeset by Litho Link Ltd, Welshpool, Powys, Wales
Printed and bound in Great Britain by Mackays of Chatham plc

Contents

To my most diligent readers and most
indulgent critics – my parents

Preface

Outsiders tend to think that corporate life is intense, strained, ambitious, deadly serious. In some measure, it is all of those things, but there are also lots of moments of humour.

(Winston Fletcher, Chairman, Bozell Europe)

When humour punctuates our working lives, we tend to look upon it as a welcome but inconsequential intrusion: a harmless by-product of the absurdities and inconsistencies of organizational life.

In truth, humour in the workplace is rarely neutral, trivial or random. It is deployed for the achievement of quite specific purposes to do with self-preservation, getting things done or getting one's way.

Managers use humour as a sword: to influence and persuade, to motivate and unite, to say the unspeakable and to facilitate change. They also use humour as a shield: to deflect criticism, to cope with failure, to defuse tension and to make their working lives more bearable. Therefore, an awareness of how humour is used, both by individuals and on them, is critical to managerial effectiveness.

Humour also plays a wider role in business, reinforcing shared values at every level: bonding teams in organizations, shaping and perpetuating corporate cultures, underpinning national management styles (especially in Britain), and even helping advertisers to segment consumers by the humorous cues to which they respond.

The aim of this book is to consider the interplay between humour, management and business culture. The role of humour in business is conspicuously neglected by management academics and gurus alike. This is an attempt to put the record straight, to expose the way humour is often at work, in both senses: to recognize the laugh that dare not speak its name.

Acknowledgements

I especially wish to thank Peter Lawrence and Carol Kennedy for their encouragement and help in the conception and writing of this book. I am also grateful to the following people who gave up their valuable time to explain how they have used humour in their jobs. Any quotations from them are taken from conversations with me, unless otherwise indicated.

Anthea Ballam, Ballam Malaguti International
Jeremy Bullmore, former chairman of J. Walter Thompson
Winston Fletcher, chairman of Bozell Europe
Sir John Harvey-Jones, former chairman of ICI
Michael Johnson, former editor of *International Management*
David Lodge, novelist
David Nobbs, novelist
Sir Peter Parker, former chairman of British Rail, and chairman of Evered Bardon plc
Eve Pollard, editor of the *Sunday Express*
Stuart Rock, editor of *Director* magazine
Sir Allen Sheppard, chairman of GrandMet plc
Tina Tietjen, managing director of Video Arts Limited
Sir Brian Wolfson, chairman of Wembley plc

Research on humour is not something about which you can be terribly up front. It needs to be observed at first hand, but to announce it as the object of one's research is asking for trouble. At best, it becomes forced and self-conscious. At worst, it dries up. So I owe a great debt to all those managers who unwittingly provided the raw material for this book while co-operating with other research projects.

Cartoons are reproduced by permission of *Punch*, Nick Baker, and Roger Beale (*Financial Times*). The Perrier advertisement is by permission of Perrier UK.

Risible
1 Assets

The essence of humour in business springs from the dichotomy between the seriousness with which business is considered and the end product. It strikes me that grown men sitting down to make up slogans for cuddly toys and so on, is intrinsically funny.

(David Nobbs, novelist)

PUTTING HUMOUR ON THE AGENDA

Apparently, making money and making jokes do not mix. Scan the index of any academic text, even the enlightened works of the management gurus, and you will be lucky to find a single entry under humour. But as anyone who has worked in an organization knows, humour plays a central role, not just in making work more bearable, spicing up office life and puncturing stress, but also in 'getting things done through other people' – as a galvanizing force, as a key to changing atmosphere and as a means of getting your own way.

This, then, is a book about humour in business. Why in business? Because business is a vast *mélange* of contrasts. And these contrasts make it a strategic site for the generation and exploitation of humour.

THE NAKED JAPE

Humour comes from hitching together unrelated ideas to form a completely new idea. Incidents and comments are only funny in a given context. Jokes are situation-specific. A cursory glance at the cartoons in business magazines reveals that much of the humour hinges on people making frivolous remarks in serious situations or vice versa. Typically, executives are shown behaving out of character or taking their executive role to extremes. Or else it is non-managers (different civilizations, children, animals) who are invested with a managerial outlook. Examples include the executive who 'holds up' his boss for a raise, the dejected director who calls in his secretary to take a suicide note, and the Viking who remonstrates with his mother that his *is* a 'proper job'. In each case, our expectations are jarred.

CONDUCT UNBECOMING

"For God's sake, Henshaw, if you're going to be an executive you're going to have to learn to make decisions."

The same rules operate in real life. Why do we often fail to laugh at the clown who falls over? Because we expect clowns to do that. If, on the other hand, we see an eminent figure, preferably a politician, take the merest lurch, the incident provokes effortless laughter. Authority has been debunked by the laws of gravity.

The idea of falling over in public can be given added piquancy in the business setting. The humour consultant C.W. Metcalf relates the experience of a female executive receiving an award at a company banquet:

> She had just reached the center of the stage when she tripped, dropped the weighty new trophy (which broke) on her host's toe, then ripped her skirt as she bent over to pick up the pieces. 'None of this would have been so bad', she added, 'except that it was an award for managing the department with the best safety record in the plant.'
>
> (Metcalf and Felible, 1992, p.41)

Humour, then, is born out of incongruity. It just so happens that business is replete with the necessary contradictions and mismatches. The serious, structured, rational side of business provides a poignant backdrop against which to set the pettiness, chaos, fallibility and uncertainty of any human endeavour. This chapter is about those inherent tensions and opposing forces – all the things which make business both difficult and good for a laugh.

RATIONALITY GONE MAD

On the face of it, there is nothing very funny at all about business. It is responsible for employment and unemployment, wealth and poverty, the prosperity of nations and the fall of governments. It has material implications for our quality of life.

That serious *raison d'être* is communicated by the language of business. It does not borrow from the vocabulary of play or biology, but from that of war. The imagery of the battlefield conveys its seriousness. Strategies are conceived, campaigns are planned, price wars are waged, and corporate raiders are fought off. Leaders are described as captains of industry, hardened managers as battle-scarred veterans, workers as foot-soldiers and the sales force as the shock-troops. The enemy is anyone who stands in the way – be it rival corporation, trade union, legislator, tax official – and victory or defeat is objectively measured by the *bottom line*. It is often said that sport is just stylized war. In the eyes of many a gung-ho leader, business is the real thing.

Pitted against this strategic hyperbole there is the mundane reality. The reality, for instance, of a recalcitrant photocopier which disobeys instructions by chewing up the master copy of a document; which mischievously delivers speckled sheets of paper instead of copies; which malevolently chops off the sides of documents it was meant to clone; which decides to run off copies of artifacts left by the previous visitor; or which disgorges 55 copies of A3 when, quite clearly, only five copies of A4 had been programmed. When routine things go awry, it becomes difficult to keep in mind the greater corporate purpose towards which we are supposed to be working.

Take the example of the three labourers working on a building site. A passer-by asked them what they were doing. 'Breaking stones', replied the first. 'Earning a living', answered the second. The third had a different perspective. 'Helping to build a cathedral', he said. Unfortunately it is all too easy to lose sight of the big picture.

One of the absurdities of business, then, stems from its intensive specialization: the fact that division of labour has been taken so far that some of the tasks people are called upon to perform would barely stretch the mind of an amoeba. And what is true at an individual or departmental level is also true at corporate level. Some companies are themselves the product of intense specialization – not just the high-tech, software-type firms, but also more prosaic businesses.

There are companies with multimillion pound turnovers which focus exclusively on branded pest control (Rentokil) or unblocking drains (Dyno-Rod) and others which manufacture toilet rolls, laxatives, or provide sick-bags for aeroplanes. This is not to deride what they do – there are times when we are very thankful for those products and services. But the thought of earnest young executives channelling their energies into the production and marketing of such offerings is bound to raise a wry smile. For example, imagine the inspired salesmanship which must have prefaced the launch of an advertising campaign based around the jingle, 'They're tasty, tasty, very, very tasty, they're very tasty.' The idea of standing up in front of hard-nosed businessmen in a well-appointed room and brazenly asking them to shell out for such creativity pushes back the frontiers of audacity.

The tension between seriousness and triviality is perhaps heightened in the advertising industry, juxtaposing as it does multi-million pound contracts and audio-visual clichés. Yet all sectors are susceptible to the same mockery. As ex-British Rail chief Sir Peter Parker commented:

Business tends to get carried away with a sense of its own importance. You get pompous mission statements and you discover that the whole point of this is making soap. Or you get gigantic technologies and they're manufacturing soup. It's enough to make God smile.

GLORIFYING THE MUNDANE

"I hear he invented the reinforced crotch."

Consider the elevation of trivia which characterized retailing in the 1980s. Business men and women became millionaires overnight by focusing on ever narrower groups of consumers. Niche marketing became the buzz concept of that decade, reaching its logical conclusion with outlets devoted exclusively to socks, underwear and ties. As David Nobbs sees it:

There is a great deal of absurdity in modern business. That aspect of business we should all respect and regard as important is where somebody makes something, which somebody else wants, and someone else is prepared to sell to them. It's when it gets to absurd levels of convolution and abstraction that it becomes worthy of scorn — where people create products to fill holes in markets and try to exploit the public.

The magazine *Punch* parodied the idea of niche marketing by reporting on 'A Success Story for Our Time' – one *SNOT SHOP*. The company's meteoric rise included an entry for 1987: 'SNOT SHOP is floated as a public company. The first floating SNOT SHOP opens in Venice. SNOT SHOP is named as the official hankie of the Olympic Games' (*Punch*, 9 September 1988).

The spoof exposed the absurdity of applying business gravitas (the notions of quality and achievement) to a frivolous product. Yet this is considered one of the keys to business success. As Walt Disney was wont to say, 'Always remember that this whole thing was started by a mouse.' The retailing equivalent, coined by Lord Sainsbury, is that 'retail is detail'. In other words, attracting and keeping customers depends on such things as keeping the shelves filled in the stores, always having enough tills manned, and so on. The notion was echoed by Ray Kroc, the founder of McDonalds, who ascribed his company's success to the fact that they take hamburgers more seriously than anyone else. An apocryphal endorsement of that philosophy came with Ray Kroc's visit to a McDonalds franchise in Winnipeg. He is said to have found a single fly. Two weeks later the franchisee lost his McDonalds franchise. Kroc's was a laudable aim viewed in terms of consumer satisfaction, but a laughable aim if one reflects on the trifling object of all that attention, the perfect hamburger.

Another example is that of British Rail. Attempts to communicate the excellence of the service to the public remained a non-starter unless British Rail could shake off its long-held image as purveyor of curled, unimaginative sandwiches. So Sir Clement Freud was asked to exercise his culinary flair on revamping the sandwich fillings. Needless to say, the fact that Sir Clement was formerly associated with the advertising of dog food was not lost on the press. It was hoped that the new fillings would finally lay to rest the jokes about the 'BR butty' which were so insidiously harmful to British Rail's reputation. The updated Intercity sandwich is now made at a £13 million plant in Wigan and transported by road overnight in refrigerated containers. Again, the resources and attention lavished on the designer sandwiches seem far removed from the basic objective of making trains run on time. Another case of disparity between a company's stated aim and the minutiae involved in achieving it that can seem absurd.

This incongruity between serious mission and uninspiring building blocks or implementation is, in fact, characteristic of any large-scale collective endeavour. Take the efforts which went into 'putting a man on the moon'. Certainly it involved endless calculations of weight-to-fuel ratios and the invention of a sophisticated life-support system; but it also meant coming up with a new form of shaver – one that was guaranteed to collect up all the bits of stubble, not leaving them floating around in the air where they might be inhaled. It also involved figuring out ways of deodorizing the unpleasant organic gases released by the alimentary canal and skin. One can imagine the party conversation: 'Gee, you're a scientist with NASA. What exactly do you do?'

This state of tension between the business's solemn purpose and the messy and mundane reality is rich in comic potential. And the fact that even those activities which we consider grand or important are reducible to the most crushing banality is what levels the playing field for humour in business.

CAMOUFLAGED CHAOS

Business is not only serious in its *raison d'être*; it is also serious in its manner. Business is an activity which is conducted in a rational and systematic way.

The structured side of business is easy to see. At an obvious level, it takes place in buildings: big, streamlined, functional ones, with right angles and symmetry, not ornately decorated or whimsically conceived ones. These buildings are divided into sections and offices in which people are meaningfully deployed on specialized assignments. This sounds like pretty arid stuff. Fortunately, the reality is rather different.

In contrast to the way they are portrayed, organizations are actually dynamic places, even in an architectural sense. Companies change premises, shut down some factories and build others. Some departments grow, often at the expense of others – Anita Roddick, founder of The Body Shop, has lamented the growth of the company's legal department in order to cope with infringements of the patent laws. Often, the only sections which stop growing in a burgeoning company are the engineering and manufacturing departments. New functions are tacked on while others are hived off.

All this movement has an impact on the office landscape. New partitions are put up, walls are knocked through, extensions are made, and hastily erected prefabs turn into permanent fixtures. Even the immutable logic of factory layout (where the machines are positioned) is subverted over time as new machines are added. A classic example is the contrived layout of the Morgan car factory – a product of *ad hoc* changes dating back to 1919. The cars have to be shunted back and forth from one work station to another, often 'swimming against the tide'. The material flow through the factory is chaotic and time-consuming. The factory organization not only inhibits expansion; it is also badly organized for the way the car is currently made. As former ICI boss Sir John Harvey-Jones pointed out in one instalment of his first six-week run as television *Troubleshooter:*

> The layout's absolutely unbelievable – and no wonder they have to start by putting the wheels on because the car's chassis is pushed up and down this hill for every additional step to be carried out. It's all money, all time and all wasted expense.
>
> (BBC2, 1 May 1990)

Companies aren't just physically structured; they are also structured in human terms. There are organizational charts, setting out the proper channels of communication for the optimum efficiency and proper co-ordination of the whole. Again, this makes the circumventing of these formal routes entertaining.

Organizations are messes of real people. Consequently the last thing that tells you how they really operate is the organization chart. People talk to whom they choose, including people they are not supposed to. For example, two friends, engineering graduates from the same university, joined rival manufacturing firms as production managers; one of them was experiencing a recurrent problem with a new production line, so the other invited him (incognito) to his firm in order to show him how they had overcome a similar problem. Rules are there to be broken. And because the rules in the workplace are more explicit than in other settings, transgression is more seductive and can seem funnier.

Managers' actions and movements are frequently trammelled by systems and programmes which govern everything from decision-making to problem-solving. Once more, the reality does not quite square up with the wished-for methodology. Too often a decision is made or a problem is solved in accordance with some rational model only after the event. It can be amusing to witness the retrospective efforts to repackage a messy, biased and ill-conceived decision so that it conforms to the prescribed procedure.

Unlike many human activities, the goals of business are articulated and quantified. Organizations set standards which they expect their employees to meet. These standards take the form of budgets, cost and profit targets and performance appraisals: clear and quantifiable objectives against which individuals, departments and companies are judged. In this respect, a group of managers differs from an informal group such as a student clique – a group whose objective, were it articulated, is simply to spend time in a socially gratifying manner. Disorder in such a group would not be funny, since that is its nature. What might be comical in an informal group would be the adoption of bureaucratic procedures or rituals.

So much for the tension between seriousness and frivolity, between structure and disorder, between the formally ordained and the informally enacted, between the august purpose and its wearisome attainment. But perhaps the biggest contrast in business is that between success and failure. Here, comic tension comes from the ease with which success can turn to failure and the efforts deployed by companies to try to insure themselves against failure.

PROFITS OF DOOM

One of the main reasons that business has plundered the vocabulary of war, as mentioned on page 3, is that it shares with war the duality of outcome. The stated intent of business is to make a profit. Everyone, from the chairman down, is expected to acknowledge that this is why corporations exist and why people work for them. If they fail to make a profit, the company has failed. Businesses are assessed on their financial performance, not on their philanthropic acts. In contrast with this 'winning is everything' ethos, business success is notoriously volatile. For instance, barely two years after Peters and Waterman published their ground-breaking bestseller *In Search of Excellence* (1982), subtitled *Lessons from America's Best-Run Companies*, a piece was published by *Business Week* entitled 'Oops!' At least fourteen of the 43 excellent companies cited had lost their lustre or stumbled in some way.

Business success is clearly a flimsy thing. The quest for success and its transience is a source of humour, at least for onlookers. Consider, for instance, the fate which befell recipients through the 1980s of the *Guardian's* 'Young Businessman of the Year' award. The fortunes of their companies were invariably transformed – for the worse. Prior to the award, every single company had easily outperformed the FT-A All-Share index, only to be subsequently humbled. Two of the companies, Coloroll and British & Commonwealth, whose bosses were honoured in 1987 and 1988 respectively, came to grief in the same week of 1990. The award seemed like a curse on the winners and their companies. Stock-market high-flyers pleaded not to be nominated.

Besides the *Guardian* nominees, a whole host of bootstrap entrepreneurs enjoyed fleeting success in the 1980s. The stock-market crash of October 1987 exposed excesses of ambition and made it much harder to finance rapid growth using firms' own appreciating shares. Profits fell, acquisitions proved unmanageable or unwise, firms became targets for takeover, and a number of the headline-grabbing figures lost their jobs, victim of their own excess. This was not just the case among niche retailers who suffered from the depression in consumer spending. Many of the advertisers, designers, stockbrokers and merchant bankers who seemed unassailable City favourites teetered and then collapsed. Their rise had been swift but, for many, the demise was swifter still.

In some cases, news of their fall from grace provoked smirks from other quarters. Understandably perhaps, for Britain 'enterprise culture' did seem to be ego-driven, the company serving primarily as a vehicle for self-aggrandizement. Retailing in particular became

personalized as never before in the UK: George Davies at Next, Sir Terence Conran at Habitat/Storehouse and Sir Ralph Halpern at Burton, all personified their own businesses. Yet their efforts (and subsequent come-uppance) paled beside the thrusting example of the flamboyant American tycoon, Donald Trump. No film star or pop personality could even begin to match his resourcefulness and determination in letting the world know of his success – Trump Castle, Trump Taj Mahal, Trump Plaza – buildings, aeroplanes and games all bore his mark. His name fetishism knew no bounds until financial crisis struck in May 1990 and it became apparent that his empire was built on a mountain of debt. The empire had to be dismembered and bits sold off. Up for sale went Trump Shuttle, the airline that carried well-heeled commuters between Boston, New York and Washington; so too did Trump Tower, the luxury hotel in mid-town Manhattan. Trump's reign as the golden boy of American capitalism was over. But even as his empire crumbled, Trump promoted his book *Surviving at the Top* (1990) – a sequel to his 1987 bestseller *The Art of the Deal*. Nero would have been proud.

How is it that Donald Trump didn't see this collapse coming? Two reasons emerge: the first was that his bankers ended up believing in the PR, and forgot to scrutinize the soundness of the mogul's operations (a mistake repeated by Robert Maxwell's lenders); the second was that Trump's downfall was not based on any one error. As journalist John Cassidy pointed out:

> Individually, the Plaza and the shuttle were risky investments. Taken together, they were a serious mistake. Add in the Taj Mahal development, and Trump's investment strategy breaches the borders of financial sanity.
>
> (*Sunday Times*, 10 January 1990, p.4.6)

Mistakes are an integral part of business life, but it is only the big ones that get exposed.

MASTERS OF DISASTER

Corporate profiles and histories are like headstones, emphatic and valedictory. Companies are portrayed as great ocean liners, making stately progress, guided by a skilled captain. They may have to negotiate the occasional iceberg, but essentially they never veer from the plotted course. Even the most diligent researcher will find it difficult to unearth the mistakes, to penetrate the detours and U-turns, for these often go unrecorded – unless of course they are on such a scale as to warrant independent media coverage.

What makes organizational bungling entertaining is again the fact that it is in such obvious contrast to the wished-for end. Business is about structured intentionality. There is a given input, there is co-ordination and there is a desired output. A foul-up flies in the face of the prevailing ethos in a way that it would not in many other contexts. To burlesque the idea, the notion of blunders in a children's playgroup is ludicrous; but what might be funny in that context would be a toddler who decided to make a speech. Relatively, then, the possibility of human error in business organizations is funnier than elsewhere because many other settings do not have the same pretensions to formal rationality.

At a higher level, corporate foul-ups become public property and can no longer be hushed up or consigned to the skeleton cupboard. These are well documented, not just by the media but also in popular anthologies of the '101 great management mistakes' variety. And these accounts are proof of a further tension in the relationship between success and failure. Simply stated, it is the ease with which failure is diagnosed after the event – compared to the difficulty of predicting it beforehand. A well-known example may help.

The story of the Ford Edsel is perhaps the classic business mistake of the modern era, the one most widely publicized and commented upon. The car's total failure in 1960 after just three years on the market can be put down to a confluence of factors. On the production side, the decision to offer an array of eighteen models and the rush to get the Edsel to market on schedule resulted in difficulties with quality control and inventory handling. The upshot was that the first Edsels leaked oil, were beseiged with rattles and sometimes failed to start – or, worse still, refused to stop (brake failure). Before these teething problems could be ironed out, the car had already become a standing joke.

To add to the production difficulties, there were also marketing mistakes. These are best divided into the four Ps of marketing theory:

PRICE: although the car was reasonably priced, Ford tried to jump the gun, by launching the Edsel early in the new model year – at the start of September – and had to suffer the consequences of competing with 1957 cars that were going through the clearance sales.

PLACE (distribution): separate dealerships were set up for the Edsel. This should have proved more motivating. In fact it proved demotivating. Dealers usually rely on the shop and maintenance sections of their businesses to cover some expenses. Not only did Edsel dealers have no other cars to work on, but the work on the Edsel was usually a result of factory deficiencies. Dealers could not charge for this work and quickly faced financial difficulties with sales not up to expectations and service business yielding little revenue.

PROMOTION: contrary to expectation, the massive promotional efforts prior to launch proved detrimental. The Edsel's appearance was one of the best-kept secrets of the car industry. The general public was led to expect the Edsel to be a significant innovation, and was disappointed by the gimmicky reality. Conversely, advertising was cut back in October and November just as the competitors were launching their new models for the season.

PRODUCT: first, the name Edsel with its ready associations with 'pretzel', 'diesel' and 'hard sell' did not enhance the car's chances. The blame here did not lie with the marketing function, which never recommended the name in the first place. It lay rather with the Ford management which disregarded market research conclusions and instead decided to pay homage to Henry Ford's only son. To add to this, the aesthetics of the car won few admirers. In particular, the horse-collar-shaped grille proved something of a turn off – almost literally, if we are to believe writer Gene Rosenblum:

The physical appearance was displeasing from a psychological and emotional point of view because the front grille looked like a high open mouth . . . Men do not want to associate oral qualities with their cars, for it does not fit their self-image of being strong and virile.

(Rosenblum, 1972, p.39)

To read this litany of miscalculations, one would assume that Ford should have seen this failure coming a mile off. How could one of the world's largest corporations have been reckless enough to go through with this project? The answer is simple. Amazing prescience is easy with hindsight. Even first-year marketing students can construct the critique of a product they know to have been an unmitigated disaster, when all the relevant information is laid out, and the case study features in the chapter on marketing. It is a different matter bringing those forensic skills to bear before the event.

Problems in real life do not come neatly packaged or conveniently labelled. They are ill-defined and unstructured. It is up to managers to discern them and prioritize them, to exercise choice and judgement. When managers take decisions they very rarely have a clear view of the situation – and one of the mistakes that academics and journalists frequently make is to assume that all the facts which subsequently come to light were available to the person when the decision was made.

Alongside Ford's textbook foul-up with the Edsel car we have more recent examples from Shell and Coca-Cola. Shell's notable *faux pas* was with Formula Shell petrol which contained a detergent intended to keep parts of the engine cleaner and a sparkling agent claimed to give better performance and fuel economy. The improvements were greeted with some rapture by the marketing men. They saw this as an answer to the problem of persuading motorists that petrol brands really were different and not just the same stuff marketed under different signs. They went to town on the promotion, only to find out after eighteen months that the product would have to be withdrawn. Unfortunately, the new improved fuel was also apt to damage the inlet valves of certain engines – thus putting paid to US $75 million of research, development and promotion costs.

Coca-Cola's major contribution to blunder legend came at the height of the cola wars. As Pepsi began to outsell Coca-Cola in American supermarkets, Coca-Cola's *éminence grise* decided to kill off its original formula and replace it with a taste closer to Pepsi's cola drink. A consumer revolt, which included the launch of a Society for the Preservation of the Real Thing, led to the company rapidly reintroducing the original product as Coca-Cola Classic.

More recently, in June 1990, Coca-Cola was forced to abandon its largest ever advertising campaign after just three weeks. The US $100 million promotion was based around 'MagiCans', which resembled normal cans of Coca-Cola Classic but actually contained money and prize certificates that were supposed to pop out of the cans and into the hands of lucky consumers. But the promotion fell flat when several of the cans malfunctioned, and consumers ended up with a mouthful of chlorinated water spiked with ammonium sulphates – not dangerous, just foul-smelling. Coca-Cola was forced to end the programme and to take out full-page newspaper advertisements warning consumers about the faulty cans.

Thus the great and the good share with the corporate minnows the unerring propensity to shoot themselves in the foot. Seeing the mighty fall, painfully but not fatally, has an appeal which is akin to the banana skin joke. The idea of self-inflicted injury is one of the mainstays of slapstick humour.

Massive commitment of manpower and financial resources, endless market research and decades of relevant marketing experience were not enough to prevent Formula Shell from misfiring, nor Coca-Cola's initiatives from leaving a nasty aftertaste. In the words of the eminent scientist Niels Bohr, 'Prediction is very difficult, especially about the future.'

DEAD CERTS

The certainty which business craves, symbolized by accountants and their terminology, wrestles with the actual uncertainty of the future. Humour feeds on the unexpected, and business is nothing, if not unpredictable.

Uncertainty springs first from within the firm. Management is about human factors. The actions, reactions and interactions of individual men and women are impossible to organize and predict with precision. People are wayward. They do illogical things for obscure or selfish reasons, as is developed and illustrated in Chapter 2.

Uncertainty also emanates from other companies. Suppliers fail to deliver, customers make unexpected requests, and competitors revolutionize markets. Invention is perhaps the most straight-forward form of uncertainty. For instance, the availability of ball-point, felt-tipped and ball-liner pens, has made the use of fountain pens almost fetishistic; and the invention of liquid detergent for washing machines sent what was already a mature market into a spin.

Then there is the uncertainty in the market. On the one hand, consumers will start buying products or services towards which they never previously showed any inclination – mineral water and recycled paper are good examples. On the other hand, they will stubbornly refuse to buy products or services that market research has shown they want, such as economy meters in cars, yoghurt or ice-cream makers, and CB radios.

MARKET FARCES

"Didn't you do any market research?"

Other examples of changing consumer tastes are visible. In Britain today, for example, there is more demand for unleaded petrol, fat-free yoghurt, low-alcohol beer, diet drinks and decaffeinated coffee than there was ten years ago – though to what extent these markets have grown naturally or been fashioned by availability and commercial advocacy is another question. The point is, though, that the product which sells today may be a Luddite joke at the end of the decade, and a market at present untapped may become saturated.

Finally, of course, companies have to contend with the environment. External influences have a habit of making a mockery of the best-laid plans. Governments change the rules of the game, resources become suddenly scarce or expensive, and stock-markets collapse. As Sir Peter Parker observed:

> You draw up momentous corporate plans, the product of much time and effort, which are taken solemnly to heart. But then if you ask people to think back to their corporate plans of ten years ago, they'd not like to be alone in the room with them. They're so embarrassing.

Businesses do their best to avoid these potential banana skins by planning. This helps them to remove or accommodate what might be termed known-unknowns. But there are also unknown-unknowns: contingencies which no amount of vigilance or scenario planning can handle. For instance, at the turn of the 1990s, Britain was blighted by a spate of food scares – salmonella, listeria and 'mad cow' disease – which affected companies throughout the food chain from producers, through distributors and intermediaries, and on to the retailers. The way these scares captured the public consciousness and the ensuing impact on sales could not have been forecast.

Examples abound of unknown-unknowns suddenly rearing up to devastate whole industries. It has often been a case of an invention coming from an adjacent sector. For instance, Keuffel & Esser, once a leading slide-rule maker, did a study of the future in 1967. This failed to foresee that within five years the electronic calculator, developed outside its business, would render its own product obsolete. Switzerland's watchmakers were similarly overwhelmed by competitors from the electronics sector. While they were developing increasingly complex mechanical watches, Japanese firms, led by Casio in 1974 launched basic digital watches which sold at less than half the price of cheap mechanical ones. Only with the introduction of the electronic, fashionable Swatch in 1983 were the Swiss watchmakers able to recapture a chunk of their birthright.

A whole edifice of internal objectives can be rendered meaning-less by a single new entrant. For instance, the mechanical typewriter industry was decimated by Japanese firms. Similarly, paperback books, video games and photocopying machines all crept to market success from alien quarters. Increasingly, estab-lished companies fall victim to the vision of industry newcomers. There is no business version of 'Trespassers will be Prosecuted'. And this complexity of context – a feature of business *par excellence* – generates humour. The misfortunes of corporate rivals – self-inflicted or otherwise – is all grist to the humour mill.

So do these daunting examples mean that companies are always necessarily prostrate before the threat of an unknowable future? Not necessarily. They can take the initiative. They can make sure it is they who 'make the going'. The best form of defence is attack and all that. But that too can have humorous consequences.

CRYSTAL BALLS-UP

The idea that 'we'd better do it to them, before they do it to us' is appealing, but fraught with danger. The problem is that there is a weak relationship between research expenditure and results – and it is not unknown for companies to bark up the wrong tree.

New products have long lead times. Thus what is true of the economic environment or of consumer attitudes today may prove unfounded when the product actually reaches the market. Today's business *démarche* may turn out to be tomorrow's sick joke, often as a result of extrapolating from the past in wildly optimistic fashion.

Steven Schnaars made a study of marketing mistakes which highlighted the propensity of companies to misjudge totally what the customer wants or will buy. Had corporate hunches been right, the world might now be revelling in bed-making machines, home dry-cleaning, showers that clean people with sound waves, foam-filled tyres, plastic teeth and tooth-decay vaccines. Meanwhile, Gulf, Standard Oil and Nestlé tried respectively to make biscuits, soups and cereals from oil.

The most bizarre propositions, however, were products of the technological euphoria of the 1960s, which emanated from the 'can do' ideology of the Apollo mission. This decade saw Ford, General Motors and Chrysler spend millions on jet-powered cars. It also saw Goodyear testing tyres with side-walls in translucent pastels under

BUSINESSMEN SHOULD BE 'BUSINESS-LIKE'

"Foster, just what kind of game plan is 'Don't Worry, Be Happy'?"

which burned a series of light bulbs – surely the product of drug-crazed minds – intended to appeal to fashion-conscious women drivers.

It is easy to sneer in retrospect but, as Schnaars pointed out, even today, laboratories are full of Cadillacs with cameras instead of rear-view mirrors, joysticks instead of steering-wheels, and GM 'night vision' aids that are cooled by liquid nitrogen.

What is amusing about all these efforts is their whimsical nature in an environment renowned for its hard-headed rationality. Business is about serious things like money and market research. In this setting, the pursuit of marketing reverie seems misplaced. We expect poets, not businessmen, to have flights of fancy.

CONVOLUTED JOKES

As if all these intrinsic difficulties were not enough to contend with, the purveyors of management practice have also been guilty of creating further complications. Consultants and academics alike have made of management something more elaborate and mysterious than it really is, leaving it ripe for debunking.

The over-elaboration is visible in the fads which regularly sweep the business community. There is humorous potential in the fickle switches of strategic thinking which see tremendous resources wasted reversing the actions of previous eras.

For instance, in the 1960s, portfolio management was all the rage, and the notion of diversification sounded too good to be false. This made for vast, multi-faceted corporations packed with unrelated products and services. The idea was that you could centralize management, save enormous fortunes with economies of scale and shelter from the economic swings which periodically hit sectors. In fact all that happened was that unwieldy bureaucracies were created, which issued memos and got in the way of the people who actually made or sold anything. The upshot was that in the 1980s many of the biggest fortunes were made by people who 'unbundled' all these pointless agglomerations.

Similarly, management has complicated itself linguistically. Originally, the growth of jargon was intended to achieve clarity. It was meant to give precision to communication in areas where the existing vocabulary was inadequate. But things have got out of control. The splintered disciplines of management – from IT and PR to HRM – are all busy churning out acronyms and buzz-words to bolster their professional standing. Like corporate magpies, they scour the vocabularies of other professions and activities for new words to appropriate. The glossaries of business terms are unable to keep pace.

The problem with EJU (excessive jargon usage) is not just that it hinders cross-functional communication, but also that it trivializes management. It suggests that management cannot stand up by itself. It makes it easy to poke fun at it, to claim, as one trade unionist did, that 'management is just common sense with a college education'. When management lays itself open to ridicule and is rightly deflated, the activity is made to look a charade. Management *is* difficult, but not in the pseudo-scientific way implied by jargon or textbooks. It is true that management has a lot to do with common sense, but managers will tell you that it takes considerable effort and skill to see to it that common sense prevails.

Once again, then, the fads, the obfuscation, the pretentiousness and bluff can be a source of amusement in a context which places a premium on clarity, logic and purposefulness.

Standing back, we can see that managers inhabit a difficult environment, one that makes heavy demands on their ability to handle ambiguity and paradox. It is an environment with progress but without direction, with structure but without order, with knowledge but without certainty. The same could be said of many human activities, but business differs from other settings in the degree of the contrasts.

Business is remorselessly ludicrous, unfortunate and tragic. If that were not enough, managers often play a large part in their own undoing. Humour springs from this convergence of tensions. It serves to expose them and to help us to carry on with all the dignity we can muster.

The Managerial Masquerade

2

Organizations exert tensions on individuals. On joining an organization you try to find out what tension is being put on you, what part you are expected to play, what role you have. And to observe people role-playing, if you detach yourself and become audience, can be very funny, because they all display varying levels of absurdity.

(Jeremy Bullmore, former chairman, J. Walter Thompson)

Business contains within its contrasts the clockwork mechanism of comedy, but it is people who put tension into the mainspring. There is quite a gap between the organization in its rational, formal plenitude and the host of wayward, imperfect human beings who staff it. Let's now unpack this tension further.

ROLLED UP IN WORK

Individuals entering companies will find that being able to do the job is not enough; they are also expected to play a role. That role is shaped by the expectations that people have of someone in that job, irrespective of who that person is. For instance, managers are expected to dress right: for men, suits are more or less *de rigueur*, unless they are entering something like an advertising agency or a software house, where the strictures may be just as severe but a lot less clear. There may be more subtle sartorial expectations: are rolled-up sleeves deemed a sign of relaxation or of getting down to business?

Behaviourally too, people in organizations have constraints placed on them. Certain traits – decisiveness, perseverance, initiative – have to be played up, while others have to be muted. The latter would include lust, envy, treachery, sloth, cowardice, greed and dishonesty, to name but some: a veritable roll-call of deadly sins. Admittedly, some of these can be revamped to look like managerially acceptable qualities such as ambition, competitiveness and business acumen – but no one likes to admit it.

Thus the contrast between the expectations that organizations have of people and what those people are really like leads to a constant mismatch which is charged with comic tension.

The idea that humour resides in the gap between an individual's outer persona and his or her real self is a long-established one. In *Twelfth Night*, Shakespeare derives comedy from the vain and pompous Malvolio who deludes himself into thinking he is the object of a young woman's desire; and in *L'Avare*, Molière pokes fun at Harpagon, who thinks he is projecting an image of generosity when his every word and deed betray his miserliness.

Contemporary examples include Basil Fawlty (*Fawlty Towers*), who sees himself as the only sane, rational person around, when in truth he is the originator of all the chaos; or Jim Hacker (*Yes, Prime Minister*), who believes he is rather adept at getting his own way, when it is he who is the guileless victim of manipulation. Both central characters assume that everyone has been taken in, when in fact they have only succeeded in fooling themselves.

To a lesser extent, the same problem confronts people in organizations. They too have to put on an act, one which befits their organizational role. At senior levels the aim is to project *gravitas*, to be seen as a person who looks, sounds and behaves in such a deeply, even heavily serious way, that everyone is convinced that he or she is a person of great depth, honour and substance: one who will deliver.

But on occasion, that mask of professionalism slips and base, non-corporate motives surface. Managers saying one thing and meaning another, managers leading each other into impossible situations, managers pretending to be what they are not, are all funny. When managers somehow give themselves away, humour, both mocking and defensive, is never far behind.

So which particular human frailties must managers overcome on joining an organization? First there is greed: not so much financial acquisitiveness, which runs parallel to the stated aims of the company and therefore offers little comic tension; more the craving for perks and the trappings of status, which is harder to reconcile with corporate objectives.

CARRY ON UP THE ORGANIZATION

The fascination of status symbols is that they have a motivational appeal which eclipses their intrinsic value. Privileges that are coveted within business, or within a particular company, may seem derisory to outsiders. But for ambitious executives, drip-fed on incremental perks, there is a massive gulf between executives who sip china tea from porcelain and those condemned to drink stewed tea from disposable cups.

The first status symbol, particularly in parts of the City where rents are highest, is space. But space in itself is meaningless if the location is wrong or if it is shared.

As a rule, an executive's importance can be gauged by his or her position on the vertical axis which links heaven to earth. Most chairmen have offices at the very summit of the building, and managerial progress up the organizational pyramid is generally accompanied by physical ascent up the building. But vertical progress is not everything. On reaching the desired floor, the horizontal plane takes over. A cramped office adjacent to the chairman's is infinitely preferable to a larger office further away.

Having acquired an office, it becomes important to furnish it appropriately. One of the reasons for resistance to open-plan offices is that they offer little scope for amassing status-enhancing paraphernalia. The first priority is to dispense with anything that smacks of functionality – metal desk, in-trays, filing cabinet – and to introduce the decorous – couch, coffee table, drinks cabinet, wall-to-wall carpeting, television set, small refrigerator, bookcase, etc.

Where functional items are unavoidable, their quality should be grossly disproportionate to their usage. Thus the boss's desk, encumbered only by a telephone and a cup of coffee, might easily accommodate a small helicopter, while the personal assistant's no-nonsense desk groans under the weight of half a ton of hardware. Similarly, the boss's chair is expensively upholstered, in spite of the fact that it sees action for barely an hour a day, while desk-bound minions spend their working lives on posture-scuttling seats. One head of department explained this disparity to his personal assistant by joking: 'If you had a comfy chair like me, you'd just go to sleep in it. What you really need is something with a spike in it, to keep you alert.'

It would appear that, where office furnishings are concerned, if you do not need it you can probably get it. And the corollary to this is that the more useless it is, the more prized it is likely to be. Thus executive office walls are lined with original works of art, desks with executive toys, and window-sills with exotic plants. The more ostentatious and esoteric, the better.

All this makes little organizational sense, and some of it is actually counter-productive. Small-time, small-minded status-mongering is socially divisive, demoralizing and likely to inhibit communication. It is at odds with an environment which prides itself on its rationality and openness. And therein lies potential for humour.

The reactions of executives in the struggle for status border on the comic. Shameful vanity and underlying insecurity are exposed. Normally cynical, intelligent men and women are reduced to trifling comparisons. The pettiness was captured by a cartoon in the *Harvard Business Review*, in which one executive warned another, 'Watch out for Pynchotte, he's getting haircuts above his level' (*Harvard Business Review*, May–June 1989, p.106).

A more familiar example is the paranoia which surrounds that ubiquitous perk, the company car. Knowing about cars has become a skill as vital as knowing about the business one is in. Corporate infighters need only take a glance at who is driving what to know how they are getting on in the company. Cars are reliable and very finely tuned indicators of status. And they are so wonderfully conspicuous. It may be gauche to flaunt your salary, but everyone will notice your company car – especially if it looks as though it belongs in the muddy fields of Gloucestershire or on a German autobahn.

For those condemned to driving practical cars, there is still the irresistible urge to wangle that bit more implied cachet: to be seen as a two-litre person, perhaps even GTi calibre. Car manufacturers naturally encourage this game, reflecting the slightest nuance of company status in limited editions and dazzling arrays of factory-fitted one-upmanship – from sports suspension to central locking, from power steering to electric windows – everything is negotiable. Even the carphone has more to do with prestige than convenience. It is a badge of office, something which tells the world that its bearer may be needed urgently and is pretty much indispensable.

Status symbols do not stop here. Anything which can be seen as exclusive, however insignificant, is something to aim for, one of the eventual rewards that makes the whole struggle worthwhile. Even something as trivial as access to the executive washroom, complete with real towels and real bars of soap, can become a major perk. And this is what is comic about executive greed and one-upmanship – not the fact that it exists, but the lengths to which executives will go in order to squeeze every last ounce of exclusivity and privilege from the most unpromising quarters.

Viewed from the outside, it can all appear quite ludicrous. As novelist David Lodge comments, 'People get drawn into the rather self-centred mystique of the professions to which they belong – and in doing so, they leave themselves open to ridicule.' Onlookers can laugh at the thought of hard-nosed executives sulking over perks they have missed out on, or jealously guarding status differentials like children hoarding toys. But not all self-serving behaviour is petty. Some of it verges on the criminal.

ALL MOD CONS

Companies expect their employees to be upstanding citizens. Yet trickery and subterfuge are criticial for getting in, getting by and getting on in organizations.

For instance, deceit of some kind is vital to eliciting initial interest from an organization. Only saints, amnesiacs and pathological liars have no damning evidence to volunteer against themselves. Selling yourself, a euphemism for lying, ranges from being economical with the truth, perhaps omitting exam failures or shading embarrassing gaps in the job sequence, right through to full-scale reconstruction of one's character and past history so that it appeals to the preferences and prejudices of the would-be employer. Hitting the right note means exuding charm and boastfulness, diffidence and brightness, all at once.

The idea is to give the impression that one is perfect for the job even if one is blatantly unsuitable. A mock advert in *Punch*, on behalf of a recruitment consultancy, lampooned the whole process:

We'll give you that indefinable 'sparkle' which sets you apart from other candidates. We'll fabricate your CV, falsifying your school, university qualifications, human rights record and sex, if need be. We'll even invent impressive new parents for you.

(*Punch*, 9 September 1988, p.12)

And reality is not standing far away. The reports prepared by recruitment consultants on short-listed candidates sometimes put estate agents to shame. The *Financial Times* reported on this practice:

Take, for instance, the one described as: 'An upright man, with a military bearing and healthy outdoor complexion.' The consultant's original interview notes on the same candidate read: 'Looks like a boozy old regimental sergeant major.'

(*Financial Times*, 3 November 1991, p.8)

Such is the extent and sophistication of written falsification in the selection process that it has spawned a profitable niche in the employment market for consultants specializing exclusively in the verification of people's career records.

The interview phase too is something of a charade. Setting aside the exaggeration of previous achievements, there is an underlying tension in interviews. On the one hand, protocol prevents candidates from asking the questions they are really interested in – about perks, time off and, most pressingly, interview expenses. On the other hand, they are required to feign desperate and lifelong interest in occupations hitherto unconsidered, the most mischievous example being the genuine query, 'So tell me, how long have you wanted to be a tax inspector?' When confronted with such an outrageous line of questioning, one is left floundering for a convincing answer. The gloss of sincerity becomes unsustainable, and humour may be the best way of extricating oneself.

Deceit of a different kind was shown by one job prospector, Eugene Roscoe, who found a way of making up to $150,000 without working (*Punch*, 16 April 1991, p.20). Roscoe was an interview specialist, applying for jobs he did not want and claiming travel expenses he had not incurred. He could hit several prospective employers from one area at a time. And if there was a danger of his being landed with the job he would, 'display a lack of technical knowledge or be obnoxious' according to arresting officer Sergeant Roy House of the Houston Police. Again, the humour comes from the derailing of our expectations.

Having conned one's way into the organization, duplicity becomes a way of life. It starts with that mainstay of organizational communication, the telephone. Newcomers are weaned on easy fibs which they deliver for the protection of their seniors: 'I'm sorry, he/she is in a meeting', 'I'm afraid I don't know his/her agenda' and the classic 'the cheque's in the post'. But they soon start to test out the device's potential for personal ends, ranging from hoax calls to colleagues to feigning illness from home.

The telephone makes it so easy to lie and so easy to avoid detection. This allows normally pleasant people to grimace, to roll their eyes heavenwards and make obscene gestures for the benefit of onlookers, while tone and inflection leave the listener blissfully unaware. And the variance between verbal and non-verbal communication can be a source of amusement for the target audience – especially when the irreverent fall foul of their own games.

At a more advanced level, the telephone offers imaginative salespeople unrivalled opportunities for deception. A number of elaborate charades were exposed in a book by ex-fraudster Harold Coyne. In one scam, a helpful colleague clicked a stapler to simulate a teletype giving up-to-the-minute market prices. In another, a salesman put his head in a drawer to recreate the echo of a gold bullion vault while giving his clients a guided tour of the depository in which their investments were supposedly lodged. Again, the tension between grandiose effect and mundane reality is both humorous and audacious.

PUTTING THE PHONE INTO PHONEY

Cupidity and illegitimate money-making manifests itself in other ways too. At the bottom end of the scale, who does not take advantage of the office franking machine and the limitless supply of free pens and sticky pads? Which boss has not, on sweeping unexpectedly through the offices, been aware of telephones being guiltily put back on their hooks? And what about the effort and ingenuity devoted to tweaking expense claims? Executives can be seen earnestly prodding away at calculators and retrospectively trying to match up the names of people who could have been taken out to lunch with receipts from restaurants where they could have been taken, on a date when they might plausibly have gone. For the more adventurous there is even the challenge of trying to get away with a birthday blow-out masquerading as an expensive attempt to keep a hot contact warm.

The scale of the fraudulence is no indicator of its entertainment value. Take the executive whose suitcase spills open in the hotel lobby to reveal an impressive range of complimentary soap and shower accessories. Such offences are insignificant, but the small-mindedness of supposedly high-minded executives is amusing. Their compulsive shady practices are comical insofar as they betray the greed and self-interest which they try so hard to conceal. Extremes of human smallness are a staple of western comedy.

If executives fall short of perfection on minor issues, they can also succumb to temptation on a rather grander scale. The 1980s saw corporate law-breaking go up-market under the label 'white-collar crime.' With information being the most vital commodity, the misuse of computers offered a whole new range of opportunities to hackers specializing in fraud, sabotage and blackmail. For others, the temptations of acting on privileged information in the stock-market turned insider dealing trials into occupational hazards.

Such crimes are not intrinsically funny. For instance, they would not be funny among inmate subcultures in prison. In such an environment, hustling and racketeering are expected, even sensible. It is often said of prisons that they are universities of crime. There is no tension between activity and environment, though there might be humour in the idea of the formalized teaching of crime. On the other hand, among senior managers who eat, drink and breathe the good of the organization, crime is at odds with corporate majesty and with their privileged positions as ambassadors of the company.

Disproportion is the soul of comedy, and the disproportion between a corporate leader's want of character and the moral stature subliminally associated with the position can be significant.

Humour thrives on that contrast between normative and actual behaviour. Writer Claud Cockburn explained:

> What arouses the indignation of the honest satirist is not the fact that people in positions of power or influence behave idiotically, or even that they behave wickedly. It is that they conspire successfully to impose upon the public a picture of themselves as so very sagacious, honest and well-intentioned. You cannot satirize a man who says, 'I'm in it for the money and that's all there is to it.' You even feel no inclination to do so.
>
> (Cockburn, 1981, p.201)

Of course, managerial behaviour is not motivated just by the accumulation of status or wealth. Sex can be another driving force. And this is another aspect of office life which involves elaborate deceits – not least on the part of the organization that pretends it does not exist.

COURTING DISASTER

People who work in organizations are supposed to leave their sexual instincts and drives at the company portals. Once inside, they cease to be men and women. They are simply staff or managers. More impersonally still, they may be referred to as IBMers or Martians (employees of Mars) – not only their gender but also their humanity subsumed by the corporate personality.

That, at least, is the theory. But of course sex is not kept out of the workplace. Enter most organizations and you enter a world of sexuality, albeit veiled. Corporate sex takes place mostly in the head. Because people are asleep for most of their time in bed, it is at work that they rehearse the mechanisms of lust and fantasy. As Gavin Ewart expressed it:

Office Friendships

Sex suppressed will go beserk,
But it keeps us all alive.
It's a wonderful change from wives and work
And ends at half past five.

(Ewart, 1966)

Passion in the workplace is not funny in itself. It is only funny in the sense that, unlike a singles' bar, the workplace is putatively sexless. Thus when there is a lapse in that denial of sexuality, there is potential for humour.

NAKED AMBITION

"I would be happy to marry you for money," she sighed . . .

The undercurrent of repressed sexuality is voiced by Philip Larkin, a poet famed for his glumness and misanthropy, who could also be something of a comic lecher:

Administration

Day by day your estimation clocks up
Who deserves a smile and who a frown,
And girls you have to tell to pull their socks up
Are those whose pants you'd most like to pull down.
(*Observer*, 28 August 1988, p.29)

Sexual fantasizing is not exclusive to men. Unattainability fuels the imagination of women too. Anna Raeburn puts the female view in a tongue-in-cheek piece from *Punch:*

Power gives a positive sexual frisson which is why, surrounded by all sorts of minor royals, gilded youth and heroes of one kind or another, the most desirable women in our modern mass media world choose businessmen.

Part of this appeal is the separation between the person he professionally aims to be and the person he really is. Neat, controlled, with rarely more than a flash of personal flamboyance, speaking in terms you don't understand and being obeyed, he takes on an aura: you find yourself adding inches to his height, fire to his eyes and wondering what he's like underneath.

(*Punch*, 24 September 1986, p.24)

The sexually charged atmosphere in offices is a natural corollary to combining three elements: mixed personnel, a high level of interaction, and status differentials. The same mix of ingredients also makes the House of Commons a sexual cauldron but is not present in, say, a theatre audience.

The sexual tension in organizations is heightened by the way they are arranged and managed. Organizations are zones of high-intensity gaze. Scanning and critical watching are legitimate aspects of the manager's checking and monitoring functions.

Avoidance of gaze in corridors is less socially acceptable than it would be 'on the street'. A degree of politeness and sociability is expected. In some positions that expectation may even be implicit in the job requirements. It may all right for a boss to be grumpy, but woe betide the secretary or receptionist who lets the facade of pleasantness fall.

Organizations also require people to meet in offices or over lunch. In these situations smiling, eye contact and sitting face-to-face are all appropriate to building a rapport and developing a good working relationship. Yet this body language is only at one remove from the signals commonly associated with sexual invitation. Even the most innocuous interaction between men and women therefore carries a sexual subtext. There is often an effort to charm the other party, if not to engage in outright flirtation. Working in an organization is generally made more agreeable by the whiff of seduction – and 'charm' is also a means of getting things done. As Video Arts' Tina Tietjen saw it, 'You are entitled to use whatever weapons you've got in your armoury. If one of them is being a woman, use it.'

Men and women, then, will trade on their sexuality to obtain information or favours which might not be so easily granted to a supplicant of the same sex. Needless to say, that latent sexuality does not always simmer below the surface. Occasionally it bubbles over. And when the carnal yearnings of supposedly blameless executives are exposed, onlookers sometimes enjoy a laugh at their expense.

Take the example of the young woman who applied for a job with a high street bank. During her interview, conducted by three men, the woman picked up a sheet of paper which one of the interviewers had dropped. Written on it was: 'Good for a screw'. It turned out to be a rare case of provable sex discrimination and the young woman was able to sue the company. The come-uppance of the guilty party allows us to smile.

There are always people who regard offices as convenient playgrounds. The office wolf feels duty-bound to smooth-talk any female newcomer with flattery and bogus lines. Other offices employ someone whose job it is to scour every utterance for innuendo. English, with its stock of ambiguous words like *it*, *lay*, *come*, *have*, is the official language of sexual insinuation – and the vocabulary of business, with its 'thrusts', and 'projections' and 'penetrations', merely adds to that supply. Every time one of these words is used innocently, it falls on the office lecher to add the predictable rejoinders, 'Say no more', 'chance would be a fine thing', 'keep your voice down or they'll all want one' – the point being that, in Britain, talking about sex is only considered funny if it is done by accident.

Others are prepared to go beyond mere words, to take chances because they think they are clever enough to get away with it. Some even enjoy the element of danger involved in riding the merry-go-rounds of promiscuity, not to mention the allure of 'sex on the premises'. Boredom, ego gratification, ambition and the inability (or unwillingness) to resist temptation, lead employees of both sexes to embark on liaisons which they may ultimately regret. Kissing couples caught in the act will spring to attention and endeavour, unconvincingly, to justify their proximity. Their explanations ('David was just helping me to straighten one of my contact lenses') have the authenticity of Groucho Marx's line: 'I wasn't kissing her, I was just whispering in her mouth.'

Organizations are popular sites for the development of sexual relationships, be they unspoken glances, mild flirtations, passionate affairs or lifelong arrangements. It is at work that newcomers to an area tend to make their first social contacts, that most affairs get started and that many individuals meet future partners.

The stereotypical relationship is between senior men (by age and status) and junior women. It is epitomized by the boss–secretary pairing, with the latter sometimes taking on the role of 'office wives', loyal and supportive, welcoming or fending off visitors, making tea, buying presents, even cleaning their bosses' false teeth (Hearn and Parkin, 1987, p.92). Deprived of opportunities to achieve in their own right, women may seek to achieve career success vicariously, through their partners. As Ros Miles wrote: 'women rarely fall for their equal at work, we're conditioned to look for men who are older, richer and more successful than we are' (Miles, 1985, p.112).

So recognizable is this pattern in relationships that humourists are able to raise a laugh by simply reversing the roles and casting the woman as the dominant party. A *Harvard Business Review* cartoon (July–August 1987, p.64) showed one such couple, torn apart by hierarchy and ambition. The man tells the woman: 'It can never work, Jennifer. You're boardroom potential, and I'm forever middle management.'

Of course, women are not always the hapless victims of crafty and persuasive male predators. Readers will also be familiar with the expression 'sleeping one's way to the top', where advances are traded for advancement. Although this is more readily associated with the casting couch of Hollywood moguls, it still goes on today, even in ostensibly merit-driven companies. A timely affair with an influential executive can help secure promotion – a leg-up for a leg-over. This is a dangerous game, however, since the merest hint of such goings-on can easily turn those involved into figures of fun, with jokes about 'getting to the top on her back' to the fore.

Adultery is one of the great themes of farce throughout the history of the western stage, and hierarchical differences add piquancy to the joke. Career success is associated, among men at least, with drive, mastery and virility. Sexual potency, we are led to believe, is directly correlated with the size of your pay-packet. Given this aphrodisiac mystique surrounding wealth and power, an easy source of humour in organizations is the self-delusion of overweight, baggy-eyed executives who publicize the constant threat to their virtue.

Naturally, not all affairs are boardroom farces. Many represent serious and demanding relationships. In any workplace, human chemistry sometimes wins. But this does not lessen the incongruity of intimacy, day-dreaming and soft-hearted sentiment in a context characterized by openness, efficiency and hard-headed logic. The idea of love among the paper clips somehow lacks romance.

Sexual reverie is just one cause of reduced work rate. And since it is partly involuntary it is also partly forgivable. But people in organizations will sometimes deliberately avoid work.

BUSY DOING NOTHING

Companies try to extract maximum effort from their executives. In many organizations, the old nine-to-five mentality has been ditched for something resembling corporate slavery. Companies expect not just involvement but commitment from their employees. The difference is neatly illustrated by the differing roles of the pig and the chicken in a traditional British breakfast. As stated in the old adage: the chicken was involved, the pig was committed. Companies, too, want their pound of flesh.

The ritual significance accorded to long hours can put quite a strain on managers. It is not enough to produce the results; people also have to be *seen* to be producing those results. This takes considerable effort. Indeed, there is irony in the fact that more energy is sometimes expended in avoiding an activity or in looking for short cuts than in getting on with it. As Miles Kington pointed out, '*Act*, can mean to do something definite. It can also mean to pretend to do something definite' (*Independent*, 14 August 1992, p.18).

Projecting a thrusting image has two aspects: the physical side and the mental side. The physical aspect is easier to counterfeit. At an elementary level it means carrying round a sheaf of papers, a personal organizer or a portable telephone, anything that suggests imminent action. It is only with experience that managers learn that the people working hardest are often those whose physical movements are only discernible with time-lapse photography.

Apart from frenetic movement, another way of indicating hard work is simply to stay late, even if it is only to chew the fat or to read the paper and avoid the rush-hour traffic. Journalist Tom Bussmann cited Major General Perry M. Smith on profile-raising:

Face time: time spent near big bosses in an attempt to impress them with your diligence and loyalty. Night face, or after-hours contact, counts double. 'Weekend face' counts quadruple.

(*Guardian*, 15 September 1990, p.3)

Notwithstanding the need to put in 'face time', it is also possible to indicate corporate commitment by proxy. For instance, one manager recalled a colleague who gave a show of conscientiousness by having two overcoats: one to wear and one on permanent display on the coat stand, thereby signalling his presence when the boss walked past his office early in the morning and late at night. Another executive spoke of a colleague who would periodically take his car to work and go home on the bus, to achieve the same effect. One is reminded of Mussolini, whose staff sometimes had orders to leave a light on in his office at night to create the impression that he was working, a dedicated servant to his people.

Mussolini also knew a trick or two about the mental aspect of appearing busy. Action, he used to say enigmatically, is desirable for its own sake even when it is wrong. He admitted that he would resort to action in moments when he did not know what to do; he had to show he was leading, and not being led, to give an impression of being always on the move and never indecisive. Managers in latter-day corporations face a similar predicament. Just as Mussolini was essentially an actor pretending to be the person the Italians wanted him to be, so managers are expected to play a certain role – and it is when we notice that they are acting, that there is potential for comedy.

We like to think of our managers and leaders getting involved, tackling or pre-empting problems, standing at the crossroads and making inexorable life-or-death decisions. This gives rise to two potential strands of humour. First, managers who feel obliged to give instant reactions will at times get things utterly, and comically, wrong. Second, managers who do not live up to the image of the executive as slam-dunking, confrontive, Gordian Knot slasher will be mocked as ditherers.

In reality, managers will shirk decisions or off-load them onto others; they will engage in tactical fence-sitting or turn a blind eye to problems. There are often good reasons for doing this, for deferring judgement until things become clearer, or even leaving problems to resolve themselves. After all, the aim of management is not to be active but to be effective. Yet fruitful inactivity is not supposed to feature in the manager's repertoire of legitimate responses. So a burst of indolence from a manager will seem funny in a way that coming from a tramp it would not.

All this concern with appearing active rather than being active, with faking rather than taking decisions, is ripe for humour. Procrastination, and the effort to dissimulate it, is funny in the

GO FOR IT!

"It was precisely this kind of indecisiveness that got us into trouble in the first place!"

corporate context in a way that it would not be funny in, say, the student environment. Students are popularly regarded as attending three- or four-year holiday camps. Indeed, students themselves play down the hard work they sometimes do. In direct contrast to the corporate environment, the best way for students to lose credibility is to be seen to be working.

This tension between activity and inactivity is one of the reasons why meetings have generated so much humorous literature.

EASY MEET

One of the simplest ways for managers to appear to be rushed off their feet is to organize and attend lots of meetings.

Meetings are reassuringly tangible in that they make it easy for managers to recall what they have done, if not achieved, by the end of the day. 'What did I do today? I attended five meetings – what a day!' With the essence of managerial work so difficult to pin down, meetings represent one of the few proofs that managers are plying their trade. After all, who on the shop-floor really believes that managers are working when they tour the works? But assemble them behind closed doors and call it a meeting and everyone will take it for granted that they are hard at work. Managers are being seen to earn their corn.

Meetings also offer the comfort of familiarity. However much managers grumble about them, meetings follow a set format: exchanges are ritualized, the participants are probably known in advance, there is often a written agenda, and there is a chance to prepare. Little wonder, then, that they come as welcome relief from the upheaval and uncertainty of life on the outside. They allow managers to slip discreetly into autopilot and periodically cocoon themselves from the rigours of having to think critically about everything they do. They are a temporary refuge from the stresses of unending and unprogrammable work. As one distribution director pointed out, 'Meetings throw up expected problems, not unexpected ones'.

The ethos of meetings is also often contrary to the idea of action and initiative. More often than not, meetings are about trivia. In part, this is because items of major consequence often have obvious answers: 'Should we attempt a hostile take-over of Shell?'; whereas issues offering little basis for choosing between them naturally provoke more disagreement: 'Should we change our little notepads for great big notepads?' or 'Should next year's desk diary be black, navy blue or burgundy?' This gives rise to Parkinson's famous law that the time spent discussing items is inversely related to their importance. Yet it is also understandable that managers tend to seize upon those issues over which they feel they have some control.

Of course, risk aversion and prudence are very much at odds with the image of courage and entrepreneurship projected in the ritualized pages of business magazines and in executive CVs. Here again, the contrast between pro-active image and actual inertia can be comical – and that tension between folklore and fact is easily exploited and exaggerated by cartoonists.

The comic potential in meetings was also explored by Winston Fletcher in his book, *Meetings, Meetings*. In conversation with the present author, he explained what he saw as the source of comic tension in that book: 'Partly it came from the ostensible aim of meetings and what actually happens in them. And partly that they're something we love to hate. Something we hate to attend, but can't bear to miss.'

This raises a final point about meetings. They are status arenas. By merely attending, managers buttress their status, while non-attendance can carry with it a certain stigma. Whether individual

TAKING CARE OF BUSINESS

NOT NOW, NOT NOW! I HAVE TO GO TO AN ENTREPRENEURIAL MEETING

managers intend to make a contribution or not, it is satisfying to be considered one of those whose views matter. Ostracism, for senior managers, is not be invited to meetings. And again, this idea of tribalistic ritual is an easy source of humour. Sir Peter Parker explained:

> If you look at the average board meeting with a picture of the chairman at the end of the room, and if you subtract the tables and chairs, everybody suddenly looks rather primitive — all dancing to a totem. There is a degree of farce and if you suddenly see it, it can be very droll.

Taking a step back, a recurring contrast emerges between human weakness and the rigid corporate roles that executives have to fill. It is precisely when people are caught misrepresenting themselves that there is the greatest potential for humour (the 'swearing vicar' syndrome). We see that behind the jet-set facade there is a tissue of shams and neuroses; that beneath the veneer of rationality and integrity there is a festering cesspool of wilful and irrelevant desire; and that flamboyant displays of purposeful action often conceal an irrepressible urge to mess around. One of the best sources of drama and humour in business is the shortfall between a manager's behaviour and his or her much-vaunted principles.

This yawning gap – between the formal appearance of rationality, bureaucratic rigour and professionalism and the imperfect reality of mendacity, licentiousness, vanity and insecurity – is exposed in all its glory at the annual Christmas festivities. This may be talked about as a time when 'anything goes'. It can be a drama of Dickensian proportions in which scenes of pride, power, lust and revenge are acted out. It is a comic drama as well as, on some occasions, an organizational tragedy.

YULE BE SORRY

Why does the office Christmas party generate so much office humour? Because it has privileged status. Most directors and senior executives are so afraid of laying themselves open to the miserable tag 'Scrooge' that they will put up with behaviour from some employees that would warrant instant dismissal at any other time of year. Employees are granted something bordering on diplomatic immunity.

There are breaches of acceptable behaviour and deportment which would normally shake the very foundations of the organization. The Christmas party, provides an annual catharsis for the passions and paranoias which lie just below the surface of everyday office life. No corporate principle is left unturned.

Business logic

Companies are built on an ethos of thrift, logic and restraint. This is in marked contrast to the over-indulgence, recklessness and lack of control that characterize office parties. Seasonal largesse is expected from the company. But such extravagance can seem indulgent in times of relative economic stringency. This is why clients and suppliers are rarely invited. To do so might simply reinforce their contempt for the company.

There is also contrast in terms of the customary respect for company property. The office, with its immaculate hierarchy of clean and decent furniture, is converted into something resembling a Marseilles dock-side dive. Party-goers push desks together, climb on them, dance on them. They spill drinks on carpets, stub out their cigarettes on them, and vomit over them.

Status considerations

Initially, the status quo prevails. Indeed, there may be heightened awareness of the differences in rank and status. Senior figures may seem a little stand-offish until they are sufficiently tanked up to mingle. Easy access to the boss at first guarantees a large crowd. Many are hoping for a casual word. But as the wine and inadmissible desires take hold, shop talk falls away and executive awe proportionately evaporates. The acolytes drift away from the once compelling centrifugal figure. A new hierarchy emerges, built on charm and entertainment value.

The group may then exercise collective pressure in getting the boss to don a paper hat, and perhaps perform some embarrassing party piece. The boss will self-consciously oblige for fear of being labelled a party pooper – and may well over-compensate on the clowning in a bid to establish street credibility. Loss of dignity is but the first casualty of the evening.

Physical restraint

Normally demure people shout hoarsely over the blaring music; those who are usually so aware of their body boundaries are suddenly given to extravagant semaphore: physical uprightness turns into slouching, sitting on floors, lurching, sprawling, wine-slopping and fumbling. Rational behaviour gives way to drunken exhibitionism, and personal space is violated with increasing frequency as the party progresses. Colleagues who would never usually lay a finger on one another slap each others' backs and hug one another shamelessly. This is no place for the sober or the dutiful.

Again, the comedy is in the contrast between activity and setting. This, explains journalist John Peter, is the conventional basis for farce:

> Farce depends for its effect on beginning in a setting of the most oppressive normality. If it doesn't, the lunatic events that follow will look merely bizarre, whereas what they have to appear is lunatic, with all the iron logic of dementia. Respectability is essential to it. The leading characters are usually middle class or above; their apparently placid and decorous existence hides unseemly urges.
>
> (*Sunday Times*, 14 October 1990, p.7.7)

Sexual decorum

The normal rules applying to office encounters are suspended as excuses for contact are proffered: loud music requires close proximity, dancing may ensue, the bright strip lights are extinguished and sprigs of mistletoe materialize.

The collective sexual energy which is normally pent up bursts forth. The chaste atmosphere of the office is swept aside by an unrestrained wave of testosterone and oestrogen. Rapacious couples are locked in soon-to-be regretted embraces.

The everyday concentration of people in typing pools, shop floors and open-plan offices is subverted as individuals seek out the building's nooks and crannies: kitchens and passageways, staircases and lifts, rearranged filing cabinets and cubby-holes serve as enclaves for private conversations. Temporary elopers cavort in store cupboards or computer rooms and find novel uses for photocopiers.

Interpersonal harmony

As the evening draws on, the enforced bonhomie may be interrupted by sporadic outbreaks of conflict. The scenario is grimly familiar. The seasoned campaigner vents his pent-up frustration at being passed over for promotion in favour of a young high-flier. This may manifest itself in a thinly veiled joke, an insult, an emptied wine glass or even a scuffle.

Not only is this yearly debauchery alien to the day-to-day idea of acceptable behaviour at work; it is also in contrast with Christmas in the domestic setting. The spiritual aspect of the season gives way to one long round of grope, gossip and gripe. Christmas in the workplace actually owes more to the pagan Viking fertility rites of Yuletide than to Christianity.

All this makes one wonder why companies persist. Christmas parties are probably responsible for more distress and agonizing, more resignations and damaged job prospects than any other single event in the corporate calendar. They are psychological minefields that are viewed by staff with a mixture of excitement and dread. Yet, as journalist Philip Norman pointed out, this makes for a compelling brew:

Office Christmas parties are invariably horrible — full of grotesque self-revelation and unwise acts and often ending in squalor, violence and regret. I enjoy them enormously.

(*Sunday Times*, 6 December 1987, p.51)

Twelve months, it seems, is long enough for selective amnesia to set in and for everyone to take their chances, once again, on the roller-coaster of merriment and disaster.

So much for the unintended humour resulting from the collision of the corporate ideal and the all too human reality. The next chapter deals with humour which has quite specific intentions.

The Dividends
3 of Humour

Humour is a way of mocking others and yourself to get the real discussion going.

(Sir John Harvey-Jones, former chairman, ICI)

JOKING ASIDE

An executive overhears the boss's personal assistant ordering something on the phone:

'What are you up to?' he enquires.
'Just getting a new chair for the boss,' answers the personal assistant.
'Good swap!' retorts the executive, feigning admiration.

The play on words pokes fun at the supposed contrast between the boss's authority and his competence. Yet the underlying implication, that the boss is useless, is too much of an exaggeration to be a valid criticism; it would be a good laugh line even for a boss who was a paragon. The joke is too detached from reality to have real bite. Its main purpose is to raise a laugh.

Further examples of humour which seek mostly to divert can be culled from office walls which are adorned with comic slogans such as 'A clean desk is a sign of a sick mind.' These pseudo-proverbs are epigrammatic and self-contained. They create playful humorous reversals of meaning out of commonly held corporate beliefs or sayings. Their rhythm and syntax give the illusion of being a popular adage or a golden rule of business. They build up tension by lulling the mind into bored acquiescence, then confound our expectations. But they are not meant to be taken seriously or acted upon. They do not really amount to a serious challenge to the dominant patterns of corporate life.

Any serious message they may hold is obscured by the anonymity of the speaker and the lack of context within which to give them meaning. Unless we know who is speaking and why, and unless the remark can be linked to a wider movement of criticism (as with, say, feminist or environmentally-driven graffiti), the humorous epigram is doomed to remain ineffective except as a source of fleeting amusement. Indeed, they are meant to be taken at face value. If they provoke a smile, they have achieved their aim. But not all humour is neutral in this way.

An unusual example was cited in an article on 'America's Toughest Bosses' from the magazine *Fortune* (27 February 1989, p.28). The piece featured one Richard J. Mahoney, Chairman of the chemicals company Monsanto. His ruthless cost-cutting in his first year spawned a wave of car stickers bearing the advice, 'Dick Mahoney before he dicks you'. Mahoney tried but failed to track down the subversive creators and distributors of the stickers.

Clearly, humour does not simply exist in business organizations. It is more than a harmless by-product of the absurdities and inconsistencies of organizational life. It is also an active agent. Humour can be *applied*, as well as *pure*. Wembley plc's Sir Brian Wolfson makes the distinction between these two forms of humour:

> You are not aware of humour when it's part of the normal flow and interchange. But there are times when you come into a situation or feel a situation begin to develop where you think, 'I have to change this' and you consciously decide that the right way to diffuse it is to crack a joke.

One occasionally comes across managers who deliberately keep comic props at hand to use under such circumstances. Among those encountered was the manager who sometimes pulled out a pair of Groucho glasses and false nose, complete with party whistle, to call a halt to really boisterous exchanges; a manager who would surreptitiously hook over his ear a small purpose-built card marked

'Bullshit deflector' to draw attention to verbal flatulence; and another who used a brightly coloured wooden popgun to shoot down people who deserved it. A more famous example is IBM UK chief Nick Temple, who is reported to have a variety of hats, ranging from Viking helmets to Napoleonic tricorns, hanging on a hat-stand in his office. These are handed out to colleagues when meetings start to become dull or unproductive (*Independent on Sunday*, 5 April 1992, p.11). Artificial though these assorted props may be, they help to change the atmosphere and dispel tension in difficult situations.

Getting things done through other people means overcoming potential conflicts of interest, clashes of personality and resistance to change. It means instilling enthusiasm, encouraging openness, and fostering teamwork. All of these can be eased with the deliberate use of humour. In its most constructive form, humour can even buttress creativity.

LARK DE TRIOMPHE

When we are trying to deal with a problem we have to distance ourselves from it. While we are totally absorbed by it there can be no possibility of finding a new attitude towards it. This is why companies often call in consultants. They come along with a fresh eye and do not take things for granted.

On a more mundane level, we face the same predicament when we try to proof-read our own writing. We are so familiar with the words that we tend to see what we think is there rather than what is actually there. That is why an outsider can come along and spot basic errors of spelling or grammar in what is supposed to be a final draft.

Humour can provide that sense of detachment. It enables us to see things afresh, to play with situations rather than get stuck with them. Humour is the mechanism which gives up rapid access to the side of our character that is more fluid, relaxed and exploratory. Humour helps to prime spirit and mind for appropriate action.

Humour and creativity have a lot in common. Both involve divergent rather than convergent thought processes: free-wheeling associations, the discovery of hidden similarities, and leaps of imagination. Two separate domains of thought are linked by a common thread which is normally overlooked, but which seems glaring once expressed. As novelist, David Lodge, sees it, 'Humour comes from surprise. What makes you laugh is something that is both surprising and yet logical or plausible.'

Consider an example. Two men are out on safari, filming a lion. As they get closer to the lion, it roars to register its displeasure. They try to get closer still. It roars again. Casually, one of the men takes off his heavy desert boots and slips into a pair of running shoes. His colleague notices and says scornfully, 'I don't know why you're bothering with those – you'll never outrun it.' The other replies: 'I don't have to outrun it. I just have to outrun you.'

The joke involves a sudden switch of perspectives of the sort that also characterizes lateral thinking puzzles. We are amazed at our own myopia, and make the smiling admission, 'I have been fooled.' 'Seeing the joke' can be equated to 'solving the problem'.

Thus, the processes which give birth to jokes and ideas have obvious parallels. Take the true-life example of senior managers faced with a problem of pilfering from lorries being loaded and unloaded. The distribution manager complains that the few cameras already in place have a deterrent effect but are actually 90 per cent bluff. So the head of production jokes, 'you might as well use cardboard cameras.' The wisecrack-cum-brainwave is enthusiastically picked up by the group and twisted, embellished and refined, but the idea of installing dummy cameras 'just for show' is finally shelved for industrial relations reasons.

A few months later a similar scheme, hatched by the Northumbria Traffic Police, hit the headlines. They unveiled a fleet of vinyl cut-out patrol cars. Designed to dissuade speeding motorists, these replicas cost a fraction of the price of the 3-D artifact (£375 compared to £28,000), and were strategically stationed in lay-bys or on bridges. As with the previous example, it is doubtful that this sideways thinking was the product of an earnest and deliberate discussion.

These two examples from the 'not-such-a-stupid-idea' school of creative thinking, demonstrate the close relationship between haha and aha. Humour can pave the way for innovation. This is not to say that a good idea needs a throw-away line to kick-start it; but an environment which is amenable to humour is also likely to be propitious to ideas, for several reasons.

Humour helps everyone relax and fosters team spirit. It promotes conditions of openness and reciprocity. An atmosphere of recrimination, or what might be called a blame culture, militates against original thought, humorous or creative. Both processes are based on introducing discontinuity, and so require the group to accept a deviation from the orderly sequence of thoughts. They also demand a certain indulgence from those listening: a readiness to pursue impulses without immediately imposing critical thought on them and to discard momentarily the constraints of logic and likelihood.

Without such an atmosphere, the likelihood of anyone voicing the crazy idea lurking in the back of their minds is minimal. There is a need to put 'on hold' the habitual fear of saying foolish things or making mistakes. As Arthur Koestler saw it, 'The creative act . . . is an act of liberation – the defeat of habit by originality' (Koestler, 1964, p.96).

So, a good way of determining whether a favourable atmosphere exists is to listen out for the level of joking. The aim is not to turn creativity sessions into laugh-ins, but a scarcity of humour may indicate a lack of flexibility, originality and comfort within the group. Creative playfulness cannot be ordained; it can only be encouraged.

Humour and creativity sometimes even combine forces (most notably in advertising). One of the most striking examples of this complicity in the business context was the apocryphal prank which won Allen Brady Marsh the British Rail account in 1979. Since it was a six million pound account, a sizeable delegation of senior BR officials, headed by Sir Peter Parker, turned up at ABM's reception. Behind the desk the receptionist was busy buffing her nails and gossiping to a girlfriend. She asked them to wait – not a thing to do with clients. Newspapers littered the foyer, ashtrays overflowed, and the coffee, when it was finally proffered, arrived in chipped cups. Finally, at the far end of the hall, double doors were thrown open and in walked Peter Marsh, chairman of ABM, and ex-actor. 'Gentlemen,' he said, 'this is the problem with British Rail. Now come next door and we'll show you how to solve it.'

This classic pitch has now passed into advertising folklore. Humour in this case was not just about being different and inventive. It also allowed the agents to confront their clients with hard truths without upsetting them.

This introduces the idea of humour as a means of probing normally inaccessible subjects. Rob Reiner's film *When Harry Met Sally* provides a neat example. Sally is complaining to Harry about the difficulties of finding an apartment in New York. Harry answers:

> That's what everybody says to me too. But really, what's so hard about finding an apartment? What you do is you read the obituary column. You find out who died, go to the building, and tip the doorman. What they could do, to make it easier, is combine the obituaries with the real estate section. So then you have, 'Mr Klein died today, leaving a wife and two children, and a spacious three-bedroomed apartment with a wood-burning fire-place.'

Humour, then, provides a channel for introducing new ideas on to the agenda and testing their validity. Humorous discourse is a means of releasing what John Kotter termed 'trial balloons'. An unusual notion, disguised as a throw-away line, can be finessed into the serious arena with impunity – that is, without ridicule or complaints of deviation from the matter in hand. But, having been aired, it cannot be erased from the collective consciousness. Insidiously, the idea firms up and may become part of the serious debate.

All this is possible because the normal rules governing serious interaction are momentarily suspended when a remark is signalled as being humorous.

UNDER COVER OF LIGHTNESS

Doctors and priests are sometimes asked for their advice in a hypothetical way. The owner of an embarrassing ailment may broach the subject with a comment like, 'Tell me doctor, suppose someone were to come to you complaining of . . .'. An alternative approach implies that the sufferer (or sinner) is a close friend with whose condition/situation one is intimately acquainted. No one is fooled, but it is accepted that normal rules will be temporarily suspended and that moral judgement will be reserved.

Something similar happens when humorous intent is signalled. Adoption of the humorous mode, like that of the hypothetical mode, gives participants a degree of protection against the negative consequences of their risky actions.

Jokers are not held accountable for their comments, so adversaries are free to make slanderous comments about each other's competence, provided these are cloaked in humour. For example, take the production director who jokes about his marketing counterpart: 'He's always looking for a challenge. Specifically, drawing a salary without doing any work.'

Or consider the exchange between two managers of different grades who unexpectedly find themselves on the same residential training course. The more senior manager asks his colleague, 'Whose rear did you kiss to get sent here?' The junior tells him, 'The list is long, but distinguished.' Humour, of a kind, was used to broach the delicate subject of ingratiation, but humour was also used to avoid having to name names. The comic interlude was immediately followed by re-entry into the serious mode. Humour, as an aside from the main discourse, need not affect subsequent interaction. It 'does not count' in the official history of the encounter.

Humorous interaction is bracketed off from normal interaction. It makes a situation explicit without risk of reprisal. And this is particularly useful in the organizational setting where the need to continually question and renew is vital to business survival.

GOING FOR THE JOCULAR

In business, more than in, say, a social context, candour is vital. The effective functioning of an organization requires people to be told when they are under-performing, uncommunicative or unwilling to delegate – and this has to be done without losing their goodwill. The 'joking mode' reconciles these disparate objectives. It can be used to deliver criticism and to stir people into action without alienating them or sapping their motivation. For instance, one managing director had systematic recourse to sporting metaphors in order to lighten criticism. Brought in to turn round a company, his first priority was to communicate his vision:

> You have to make sure that everybody understands the rules you are trying to play to and why, the dimensions of the field and how you count the goals for or against. And there was a lot that needed sorting out, because half of them thought they were playing cricket, and others thought they were playing football, but weren't sure which way they were kicking or which half it was.

He went on to explain:

> I use sports analogies quite a lot in describing things to people in the business. I find that most people have a passing interest in one sport or another – and once you understand what it is, then you can usually find suitable parallels. It also depersonalizes criticism. People can readily understand if you tell them, for example after a psychometric test, 'I know you want to be an opening bat, but frankly, I think you are a better leg spinner, and that's where I see your role.' If, instead, you say to them, 'You've had your psychometric test and it shows you're an introvert', they'll take exception to it. They'll deliberately go out of their way to prove they're not – and will probably make a mess of things.

Humour, then, can be used to deliver unpalatable messages or potentially unpalatable messages with a softened impact. Most commonly, this takes the form of teasing.

Teasing is something you do to others. It is never self-administered. It is a way of censuring others by letting them know you have noticed, without actually telling them off. For instance, a supervisor who chances upon a group of workers taking an extended tea-break may warn them, 'At this rate, they're going to have to start docking tea-breaks from holiday entitlement'. It is a mild rebuke in a situation where open criticism or a formal warning is deemed inappropriate; it is especially useful for the early prevention of problems. The teaser gently admonishes the mis-creant without making a big fuss – and custom forbids the person on the receiving end from taking offence.

Teasing is particularly prevalent in meetings, where the con-tinued contribution of all participants is important. So rather than condemn a long-winded manager outright, one director preferred to marvel at the fact that 'he hasn't drawn breath for five minutes!' Another director, referring to a subordinate's fairly lame excuse, remarked, 'That was about as convincing as Dick Van Dyke's cockney accent.' Or again, a head of department told one of his junior managers, 'We're going to have to start calling you Teflon' to draw attention to the latter's repeated deflection of responsibilities. Similarly, when two individuals showed that they were intent on scoring cheap points off each other, a simple prod from the chairman, 'Seconds out, round two', was enough to disarm them. As Jeremy Bullmore points out:

> In meetings where tension is building up and the sense of opposition is greater than the issue demands, then humour is often the best way to puncture that. It can allow both sides to realise they're getting overconcerned about something quite trivial. They can feel foolish. They can join in the laughter. And you can smother the situation that way.

Teasing, then, is a discrete way of sanctioning deviant behaviour. It requires the 'guilty party' to laugh at the tease, thereby acknowledg-ing the deviant action, but it also allows him or her to rejoin the group without losing face. Typically, when someone arrives late to a meeting, teasing is used to mark the violation while quickly returning to a state of consensus among those present.

Teasing is not just about chiding. It is also used to draw people out of themselves: to goad people into action, to chivvy them along or to push waverers gently off fences. This is often achieved by mimicking their timidity or evasiveness: 'Is that your final indeci-sion?', or conversely, by exaggerating it, along the lines: 'If the rest of us can get a word in ...' As GrandMet's Sir Allen Sheppard observes. 'Teasing is a way of getting people to open up and realize that they should contribute, and not be inhibited by the fact that they might have two levels of bosses there.'

Sir John Harvey-Jones also saw it as his initial weapon against fawning: 'Teasing helps to eliminate undesirable creeping – if you knock it once or twice, then people tend to desist.'

An example was the managing director who, weary of hearing one manager drop acronyms and buzz-words, suggested he'd better lay off the alphapet soup for a while.

Of course, humorous criticism is not confined to teasing. It can take rather more pointed forms – particularly where upward criticism is concerned and teasing is less appropriate. As Sheppard puts it, 'If individuals want to be fairly fundamentally critical of some aspect of the company they need to find a way which doesn't actually bring the conversation to a halt. Humour is the key.'

THE TRUTH SOMETIMES HURTS

WELL DONE, IT HAD TO BE SAID

One secretary, whose boss had asked her to pour the tea she had just brought in, retorted, 'Would you like me to drink it for you as well?' Another secretary, asked by her boss to dig out a copy of her job description, queried, 'In the mood for a bit of fiction, are we?' A third secretary made up a card of the 'Do not disturb' variety which she hung on her bad-tempered boss's office door. It read: 'I wouldn't go in there.' In all three cases, the point was taken, demonstrating that humour is one of the few available channels for conveying hard messages upwards.

Or take the case of a middle manager who failed to receive his long-awaited salary upgrade on account of the company's straitened circumstances. Asked for his reaction by his boss, he pulled no punches: 'I am very bitter and twisted about it all.' Using humorous exaggeration he could be forthright without actually impairing future relations with his boss.

A similar effect can be achieved with humorous imagery. A memorable example was the reaction of a personnel director to his boss's proposal that they reshuffle middle management responsibilities: 'You don't get a better brothel by shifting the beds around', he explained. 'You've got to change the girls.' The implication was that it would take more than cosmetic changes to improve middle management.

In another instance, the managing director of a brewery asked his assembled managers whether the solution to slimming the workforce might be to put up a note asking for volunteers for redundancy. The foolishness of the suggestion was cheerfully exposed by the production manager with a graphic warning, 'You'd be crushed in the stampede.'

Humorous imagery of a distinctly tangible kind was effectively used in another context. The person on the receiving end was an executive who, having committed a rather underhand manoeuvre, later returned to his desk to find a knife smeared in ketchup. Beside it was a note saying, 'I found this in my back. I believe it belongs to you.'

Thus humour can take the sting out of criticism. But it can lower individual resistance in other ways too; it helps to accelerate understanding and makes people more amenable to persuasion.

LAUGH AT FIRST SIGHT

Business organizations are characterized by their hierarchic nature and their competitive ethos – between individuals, between departments and between companies. Consequently relations within business, particularly between new acquaintances, are marked by a certain wariness and suspicion. People are not as candid and spontaneous as they might be socially because they have a particular rank, responsibility and workplace persona to uphold. These tend to induce feelings of pomposity, rigidity and a corresponding loss of human warmth and open communications. Humour serves to restore these qualities, helping to establish a rapport and nurturing an environment of openness and trust in which discussion can move forward. As Sir Brian Wolfson put it:

> The use of humour between strangers is about breaking down barriers and establishing an intimacy – temporary maybe and false over time – but which allows you to do things in a short time which would otherwise take a long time.

As managers rise up through an organization they gradually lose touch with what is going on near the base. They have to devote more time to external contacts. They cease to use the same facilities – coffee rooms, washrooms, canteens. A lot of potentially useful information is filtered out or 'dressed up' before it reaches them. And when they do manage to squeeze in a tour of the workplace, staff are all beaming smiles and best behaviour.

Given this restricted contact, it is vital for top managers to put people at their ease quickly and to remove the inhibitions of relative status. Managers can use humour to establish a rapport, to communicate their openness and robustness, and to draw out the genuine feelings of their juniors. A hotel general manager explained the predicament:

> Something that did not strike home until I had been general manager for several years, is that you are at the top of your little pyramid. So everybody smiles at you. They all present their nicest sides, as I would to my boss. You can sometimes use humour to break through that facade and find out their real concerns.

The director of an insurance company confirmed this view and explained how he set about breaking the ice when inviting groups of junior staff for informal chats:

> If, after fifteen minutes, they are still playing around the edges, which is often the case, I'll tell them, 'You're the easiest lot I've ever had. Why don't you ask me something awkward like how much I earn, whether we're going to make any redundancies, what about the pay deal?' and away they go.

He went on to explain, 'I want to know what they're really thinking. And they might not otherwise ask potentially embarrassing questions to a senior manager, if I didn't open up the way with humour.'

Humour, then, can be used to express willingness to listen to staff fears and concerns and to be put on the spot. It is self-revelatory and conveys sincerity, which encourages others to drop their guard. Far from being a time-waster, humour can help to draw out information which might not otherwise be volunteered. An operations director explained:

> Your sense of humour says a lot about you. If you allow it to show through, you betray something of yourself, but you also find out a lot about the person you're talking to. By delivering who I am very quickly, I find that makes it easier for me to read other people.

A timely dash of humour quickly puts people at ease and dismantles interpersonal barriers. It paves the way for more open, frank and constructive discussion. Humour is a way of getting people into a rosy frame of mind without heavy expenditure on alcohol. Or, as one chairman who shall remain nameless suggested, 'Humour is the Vaseline of corporate intercourse.'

Dealings in humour

One person noted for his use of humour as a lubricant was Henry Kissinger. Richard Valeriani, a dedicated Kissinger-watcher explained:

> He made humor a tool of diplomacy. His banter inspired banter in others and usually led to a more relaxed atmosphere in the private, formal discussions or negotiations with world leaders. The humor opened the door to more frankness and less ritualized recitations as well. In that regard, Kissinger lightened the whole heavy international diplomatic scene.
>
> (Valeriani, 1979, p.9)

Most types of business activity involve some form of negotiation, even something as routine as when and where to meet for lunch. Humour can establish a constructive climate for negotiations. It allows managers to be tough and firm without being abrasive. Comedian John Cleese explained the persuasive power of humour in negotiation:

> If I can get you to laugh with me, you like me better, which makes you more open to my ideas. And If I can persuade you to laugh at a particular point I make, by laughing at it, you acknowledge its truth. It's no coincidence that the man I know who always has the best stock of new jokes is not a comedian, but a salesman.
>
> (*Wall Street Journal*, 1 August 1988, p.1)

Sir Allen Sheppard went along with this view, explaining, tongue in cheek:

> Humour is a way of relaxing people. If you get into a tough negotiation with a person, if you can get them to smile or laugh, you'll probably get a lower price . . . and if you can make them cry, you'll probably get a lower one still.

The use of humour in negotiation is particularly relevant in Britain, where the system of industrial relations is based on horse trading, muddling through and personal relations with the shop stewards. Humour can be a useful device for bridging class gaps with workers and removing the idea of 'them and us' which is especially harmful to labour/management relations.

Take the proposed restructuring of the system of sick pay in one firm. The company's management were keen to discourage uncertified sickness and to be more generous to those suffering long-term illness. Naturally enough, the trade union representatives wanted the best of both worlds and put forward a proposal to that effect. The personnel manager tapped out some figures on his calculator, then announced apologetically: 'I'm sorry, I can only get eight digits on my adding machine'. He made it plain that what they sought was unreasonable, but did not antagonize them by telling them, 'You must be joking'. He thus confirmed that confrontation in negotiation is more about *how* things are said than *what* is said.

Humour, then, is sometimes suited to negotiation because it provides a channel for making oblique statements which avoid head-on assertion. For instance, one director's assurance that management would not give in to trade union demands was rounded off with the qualification, '. . . and I am unanimous in that.' This emphasized a determined stance without bringing the whole discussion to a close.

And when one side is being obstructive, humour can break down that resistance in a non-conflictual way. For instance, Norman Willis, leader of the TUC, was presented with a problem during negotiations with the employers. Not wishing to be sidetracked from the main issue he gently dismissed the matter, saying, 'We'll jump off that bridge when we cross it.'

But humour is not just used to build bridges and sidestep confrontation. It can also be used to shake up the rigid negotiating process, as revealed by Sir Peter Parker:

You can use humour in negotiation because it is generally unexpected. If people are all set, considering their affairs and their PR-polished phrases, an injection of humour brings an element of surprise to the situation. And it makes it more difficult for people to plod on with their rehearsed arguments.

In one instance, shop stewards were demanding concessions which seemed blatantly unrealistic. Momentarily subverting the stereotypical stances, the head of department chairing the negotiations turned to the shop stewards and asked, 'If you were the manager, you'd be quite happy with what you're telling me, would you?' The two shop stewards looked at each other, then broke into broad grins in spite of themselves. The use of hypothetical role-reversal brought out the absurdity of their suggestion. Had they not laughed, they would simply have looked stupid. Humour can help to shame an adversary out of a position which no amount of argument could make that person abandon.

So humour can serve as a form of ambush in a negotiation. Adversaries can be unsettled by disrupting the normally well-choreographed pattern of exchange. Indeed, there is an interesting parallel between comedy and negotiation in that they both rely on the order in which information is disclosed.

The dual uses of humour in negotiation – to foster bonhomie and to seize the initiative – come together over a business meal.

YOU MAY SCOFF

Being merry is a natural corollary to eating and drinking. Humour tends to flourish during business lunches for a number of reasons. Eating is a convivial affair. Like humour, it is a shared experience. In the peace and intimacy of the restaurant business can be conducted graciously, at a leisurely pace, and diluted with social conversation to ensure that both parties are at ease. There are no operational pressures with which to contend or distracting faxes waiting to be answered. The participants can relax and, unfettered by organizational constraints, their minds can range freely. There is no set agenda, no urgent deadline. The conversation can digress, and appropriate anecdotes can be trotted out.

The convivium is reinforced by the physical proximity of the protagonists. At table, the parties shift from a desk width apart to within touching distance – in other words, from a work relationship to a social relationship. This facilitates communication both psychologically and physically. The actors can see and hear each other perfectly and non-verbal communication is less theatrical. Self-presentation is easier and anxiety is lowered by the physiological effects of eating and, of course, drinking.

HUMOROUS REVELATIONS MAY ENSUE

"I'll level with you, Fairweather. I don't really speak French."

In this conspiratorial environment the participants are more likely to let slip humorous indiscretions and to allow their real comic persona to shine through. This is not just the liberating effect of alcohol. It is also a product of the ethos of business lunches.

Business lunches are not primarily about selling the company or its products and services. That can be squeezed in at the coffee stage. Lunches are about putting on a good show, about convincing the other party that doing business together would be fun. There is a premium on repartee and levity. And, contrary to popular belief, managers are often genuinely interesting people. They travel all over the place, meet different people and argue, persuade and analyse. They sack and get sacked. Their personal skills are finely honed; they are funds of practical observation and anecdote; they are broadly cultured. The business lunch provides an opportunity to put this wealth of experience to play – to soften up the adversary for the kill.

A week after their meal, the participants will have little recollection of precisely what was said. The content will fade but the two parties will recall how they felt. Humour helps to create a positive relationship, and *that* will be remembered.

The power of humour to lower resistance to persuasion also extends to the corporate classroom.

PLAY AS YOU LEARN

Management training was long thought of as a most serious and sober undertaking. Instruction material for business and industry was not noted for its entertainment value. In recent years, however, humorous training videos have made considerable inroads into the traditional fare of manuals and textbooks, cassettes and films.

John Cleese is often cited as the father of the humorous video. It was he, in conjunction with Anthony Jay, Peter Robinson and Michael Peacock, who launched the Video Arts Company in 1972. One of the guiding principles of the company was that it was possible to encourage desirable behaviour and promote techniques by disguising instruction as entertainment. Comedy is used to teach managers professional skills and tasks as diverse as chairing meetings, negotiating contracts and selecting staff.

This use of comedy as an attention-grabbing device is not universally accepted, however. There are those who argue that the comedy interferes with the message, that the gain in learning due to attention-grabbers is offset by the fact that the message itself is overshadowed. John Cleese himself concedes that this can be the case if the humour is not carefully integrated into the management lessons. On the other hand, where the humour encapsulates the teaching points it is impossible to remember a 'joke' without also recalling the attendant lesson. Concept-related humour, as it might be called, is vital to the effectiveness of information acquisition and, perhaps, more importantly, to information retention.

Provided that the humour *does* arise from the training points, there are two further advantages to incorporating humour in training. First, simply receiving a clear message does not necessarily mean agreeing with it. The aim of the teacher is to persuade – agreement, not reception, is the principal objective. And laughter marks a specific acknowledgement of a learning point. So when individuals hear others around them laughing, the lesson is reinforced by the peer-group reaction. Second, a humorous lesson affects us in a way which differs radically from a straight lesson. As John Cleese explains:

> Our behaviour is seldom changed by a simple verbal instruction. Such instruction goes from one intellect to another and does not affect us at the gut level from which our behaviour arises. The point of comedy is that it involves an audience.
>
> (*Wall Street Journal*, 1 August 1988, p.1)

This is an interesting point. Humour does implicate us. It draws us into mental collaboration. In order to 'see the joke' the viewer has to fill the gap – a joke is never fully explicit, otherwise there is no sense of surprise and thus no joke. Consequently, when the point of a joke is explained to us, we do not feel gratitude but resentment. We have been denied the chance to contribute. As Jeremy Bullmore saw it:

> Involvement seems to me to be everything in communication. If I do everything as the sender, the only thing left for the receiver to do is to refute it. Because the only contribution you can make is to disagree with me.

Setting the foregoing arguments about the effectiveness of humorous messages aside, there is another critical point, and one which tends to be overlooked. Simply stated, it is that humorous videos are hugely popular. Perhaps, all things being equal, a straight message would be better assimilated. But the fact is that people who would never have watched, uncoerced, a conventional training film on, say, safety at work, will flock to see the comic version starring Rowan Atkinson. British managers, who have never been noted for their devotion to training, have found a way of educating themselves painlessly.

There is a final strand to the argument that humour lowers resistance; it is that humour can lower media resistance to corporate propaganda.

SHOOTING FROM THE LIP

The relationship between a company and the Press can be enhanced by banter. For instance, PR agency head Anthea Ballam is quite calculating in her use of humour with journalists:

> As PR people it's our job to be very polite to journalists so that they'll write about our clients. So one of my techniques is to do the exact opposite, that is, to be extremely rude to them and quite offensive. And they seem to find it terribly funny because they're so used to being treated with kid gloves.

This confirms the idea that humour comes from acting out of role. In this case it is done deliberately, for comic effect, rather than inadvertently. But the result is the same. It produces a state of tension between actual and expected behaviour. Anthea Ballam does not fawn but pretends to bully instead – 'Okay pin-head, just do what I tell you to do and write about my client' – thereby generating humour by subverting the stereotype of the obsequious PR person.

Besides helping to handle reporters, humour also serves as a means of making one's point in an age when we are bombarded by sound-bites. Consider the example of John Prescott, then Shadow Transport Secretary, on the *Today* programme (Radio 4, 3 October 1990). He was deploring the state of Britain's railways and the fact that British high-speed trains ran at speeds of 50 to 100 mph slower than their continental equivalents. He rounded off his assault with the observation that, even at this snail's pace, British trains 'couldn't keep the coffee in the cup'. It encapsulated his argument and left an enduring impression on the listener.

Dennis Skinner, the irreverent Labour politician, is also a proponent of this tactic, explaining:

> I've never gone in for ribald comments for the sake of making them. I believe you can fashion words in a way to get a message outside which will have a political content, and that's what Parliament is there for, to get a message to the outside.
>
> (*Sunday Telegraph*, 2 February 1992, p.III)

Some company heads, too, have a knack of presenting information in a comic or pithy way which makes it irresistible to the press. For instance, there is a saying among financial journalists that when a piece lacks punch, they just need to talk to Sir Allen Sheppard for about five minutes in order to come away with a ready-made headline. Sheppard says that this is not conscious, and modestly claims, 'It's just that I talk in picture language because I'm not bright enough to talk in any other way.'

An example of this picture language, and one which is frequently cited, is the 'light grip on the throat' style of management. This striking image was the result of a spontaneous answer to the question, 'What do you do if managers don't perform?'

Sheppard relates another interesting example of the far-reaching power of snappy replies:

> I'd been Chief Executive for about thirty seconds, and Lisa Wood of the *Financial Times* asked me, 'What's wrong with GrandMet and what've you got to do to put it right?' I answered, 'We've got a cluttered business portfolio.' So she said, 'What are you going to do about it?' Short of giving her a three-day presentation, I just said, 'Well, I'm going to de-clutter it.' Then everybody started to use the term de-clutter — this was before unbundling became the rage — and we therefore decided we'd use it to rename our own corporate programme.

This timely piece of demystification served as a memorable rallying call for the new business strategy, making it accessible and giving it focus and momentum – thus demonstrating that the humorous message is not just aimed at outside constituencies (investors, consumers, competitors) but also at employees.

Exploiting the press to reinforce corporate values is one tactic which is particularly dear to Amstrad chairman, Alan Sugar. He too employs a rich line in off-the-cuff phrases to woo the press – and to hammer home the idea that Amstrad is essentially a marketing company.

Sugar has boasted, for instance, that he would sell portable nuclear weapons if there were a demand. And to communicate the idea of relentlessly pushing down the price to meet the mass demand, he claimed, tongue firmly in cheek, that he made factory rounds clutching a pair of cutters: 'If I find anything that costs more than a couple of quid, I snip it out!' (*Reader's Digest*, May 1988, p.44). One was reminded of Sam Goldwyn's famous line, 'Spare no expense to make everything as economical as possible.'

Amstrad then, is driven by what sells, and Sugar is constantly reminding people of that via the press. But he eschews the conventional inanities about satisfying consumer needs. Instead he tells reporters:

> If it's the difference between people buying the machine or not, I'll stick a bloody fan in it. And if they want bright pink spots on it, I'll do that too. What is the use of my banging my head against a brick wall and saying, 'You don't need the damn fan, Sunshine'?
>
> (*Financial Week*, 1 October 1990, p.31)

Perhaps his best-known comment, however, was made in a speech to the City University Business School in May 1987: 'Pan Am takes good care of you. Marks & Spencer loves you. Securicor cares. IBM says the customer is king. At Amstrad we just want your money' (*Independent on Sunday*, 27 September 1992, p.6). Corporate sloganeering was thus mocked, but Amstrad's self-image, as a company which bucks the trend, which is realistic and decisive, was bolstered.

Of course, using humour carries a risk. Sir Allen Sheppard was once quoted as saying 'Any executive who can't punch me back in the face isn't worth hiring.' One reporter took exception to his flippancy and branded him a misogynist. Sheppard promptly wrote back saying that some of the most lethal punchers he'd met in his life had been women – thus demonstrating the use of humour to get out of a tight spot. But it is not always so easy, and those dealing with the press must be especially mindful of the limits of humour. The ignominious fate of Gerald Ratner should serve as a warning to those intent on living by their wits.

REVERSE ALCHEMY

Picture the scene: Gerald Ratner, then 42, and one of Britain's best-known businessmen, was landed with the tail-end slot at the annual convention of the Institute of Directors in London. Such heavy-weights as the Chancellor of the Exchequer, the Institute's Director-General and President de Klerk of South Africa numbered among the previous speakers that day. And by the time Gerald Ratner took the rostrum, the seven-course lunchbox and brandy chaser were taking their toll on the 3,000 company directors. It was going to take something pretty spectacular to gain the attention of these punters. But Ratner succeeded.

Blithely describing one item of his own merchandise as 'total crap', he drew enthusiastic cheers from the Albert Hall audience. Encouraged, he continued:

> Some people say they cannot even see the jewellery for all the posters and banners smothering the shop windows. It is interesting, isn't it, that these shops that everyone has a good laugh about, take more money per square foot than any other retailer in Europe. Why? Because we give the customers what they want.

Then Ratner went for the kill: 'We even sell a pair of earrings for under £1, which is cheaper than a prawn sandwich from Marks & Spencers. But I don't have to say that the earrings probably won't last as long.' The audience loved it.

Unfortunately, less than three hours later, his comments were already running in the late editions of the *Evening Standard*. On the following day, the tabloids created a furore: 'Rotners' barked the *Sun's* front page; 'You 22-Carat Mugs' was the *Mirror's* uncompromising headline.

How could he have committed such a gaffe? How could one of the country's most successful retailers have blundered into a minefield of adverse publicity?

The answer is quite simple. Ratner had made the fatal error of taking a private joke public. A light-hearted aside that went down rather well with financial journalists and City advisers spelled disaster in the hands of hungry newshounds.

The irony was that these remarks were not just shop-soiled but had actually found their way into the *Financial Times* as far back as January 1988. The prawn sandwich quip was so old that it was virtually a company motto. The comments simply had not been picked up by the tabloids.

Much of the credit that Ratner had painstakingly built up with customers for giving good value and making jewellery affordable was wiped out with a few one-liners. He had single-handedly revolutionized the marketing of jewellery, exploding the mystique surrounding stuffy jewellery shops; then he single-handedly shot the golden goose.

A year later the company was still smarting from his injudicious use of the C-word. The group's share price was languishing at around 15p, from 150p just twelve months earlier. Eighteen months later he bowed out of the company altogether, having previously relinquished the chairmanship to Jim McAdam, former head of the textiles group Coats Viyella.

CHEAP LAUGHS

There are a number of important lessons to be drawn from Ratner's undoing, not just to do with humour in business but also concerning the nature of business.

Ratner's was not a mistake in an absolute sense; after all, the throw-away line had entertained people before, and with 99 per cent of the audience it also worked on the day. This was an error of judgement.

As with comedy, the first rule of humour in business is timing. There is a time and a place for humour. It should be geared to the audience and the occasion. With the bulk of those invited to the Albert Hall, Ratner was probably on safe ground, in that they were unlikely to be frequent visitors to Ratner's cheap and cheerful stores and therefore unlikely to take offence. If anything, his comments would probably elicit a mild feeling of superiority from them. Humour helped Ratner connect with them, by distancing himself from the goods he sold and establishing shared taste. But Ratner seemed to overlook the fact that, for an influential minority of those attending, his statement represented far more than just a good laugh.

Imagine what it must be like for a hard-bitten reporter to be asked to cover a business conference instead of chasing ambu-lances or doing some investigative sniffing. What, until then, had been a fairly tedious event suddenly turned into a dream assignment, bursting with seductive phrases, variations on the theme of 'All that glitters is not crap'. This promised to be a field-day for headline writers and cartoonists alike.

COMIC GEMS

"Our jewellery has really hit the fan!"

The presence of the media changes any occasion. So if in doubt, managers should try to visualize the proposed comment being broadcast out of context on television or plastered over tabloid newspapers. Managers in the public eye have to try to develop a hindsight mentality, the only problem being that excessive reflec-tion and caution will always militate against humour, thus depriving managers of a valuable tool. The critical questions when determin-ing whether to use preconceived humour in a public forum are:

1. *Is it funny?* Not just for the individual, but to that audience? In other words, does it achieve the tricky combination of familiarity on the one hand and surprise on the other?

2. *Is it pertinent?* That is, does it reinforce the message, or does it serve as a 'listener reward' to refresh the audience? If it does neither it is merely a hostage to fortune.

3. *Will it offend?* One must know one's audience. The less homogeneous that audience, the more care needs to be taken to avoid offending some faction. And it only takes one person to change the nature of a whole audience — if the Pope happens to be that person. One way to avoid causing offence is to mock oneself, provided that it does not undermine one's credibility.

Seemingly blessed with the Midas touch, Gerald Ratner perhaps felt in a strong enough position to risk jokes about his cut-price empire. That would have been fine, provided the humour had been self-deprecating. But he was not the target of the joke. Ratner broke the unwritten rule of business when he insulted his customers – and paid a heavy price for laughing at their expense. As public penance, he was obliged to absorb any amount of abuse that was thrown his way.

His fate also illustrates two of the themes covered in Chapter 1 of this book. First, business success nurtures the seeds of its own downfall. Gerald Ratner had achieved the notoriety and exposure which amplified any public statement he made, thereby giving rise to Ratner's law: *Anything you say in public can and will be used to mock you and your company.*

Second, it is easy to be wise after the event. Had it not been such a slow news day, he might have got away with it. His comments would have received the attention they deserved, tucked away in the anecdotal rubric of the City pages. They would merely have bolstered his image as an anti-establishment figure. He was unfortunate in being the last turn of the conference and in trying too hard to please the crowd.

With hindsight, it is easy to see what Ratner did wrong; yet his assertion was not so distant from Alan Sugar's celebrated claim: 'At Amstrad we just want your money', which earned *him* favourable coverage among the quotes of the week in the Sunday broadsheets. Again, this exposes the tightrope which business people walk between success and failure.

MISSING BY A SMILE

Humour is neither good or bad. It is a tool at the manager's disposal. One consultant remarked, 'It's often said that if you have a hammer, every problem looks like a nail. Humour can give you that extra dimension to tackle a problem differently.'

Used judiciously, humour defuses tension, rallies the troops and moves the organization forward. But it has its limits. For instance, humour is better geared to conflict reduction than actual resolution. Thus it can be used to suppress feelings of anger which need to be met head-on and thrashed out. If humour is merely used to side-step a recurrent source of hostility, the likelihood is that it will simply surface later in a destructive fashion. Similarly, when there is an emergency and precise action is urgently required, humour is not recommended. As John Cleese explained:

> If you want a decision in two minutes, don't open up the discussion. When you charge the enemy machine-gun post, don't waste energy trying to see the funny side of it. Act narrow-mindedly.
>
> (*Wall Street Journal*, 1 August 1988, p.1)

There is a Gary Larson cartoon which illustrates this point well. It features a scientist with a white laboratory coat carefully working on the delicate internal wiring of a large atomic missile. Behind him is another scientist with a big grin on his face, a blown-up paper bag in one hand, his other hand poised to pop the bag.

The appropriate use of humour does not lend itself to join-the-dots prescriptions. It boils down to managerial sensitivity, to individuals and occasions. As humour consultant, Malcolm Kushner, puts it, 'Each interaction with other people requires you to assess the situation from a fresh perspective. You must recognize individual nuances, make adjustments, and use good judgment' (Kushner, 1990, p.121).

For instance, lack of sensitivity was demonstrated by the director of a large publicly quoted company who, in a spirit of bonhomie and goodwill, decided to send out for ice-creams for the 400 staff of a particular unit. Coming, as it did, just weeks after an unsuccessful round of pay negotiations, the symbolic gesture did not quite have the anticipated morale-boosting effect. Staff reactions ranged from 'I suppose this is going to pay the gas bill' to 'He knows what he can do with his cornet!'

Just like management itself, humour is about judgement.

Who Laughs
4 Lasts

In a reactive sense, humour is a way of coping with adversity. When things are prosperous there's little humour about. People are too busy trying to make a living. But when there's a reverse . . . like Black Monday . . . within 24 hours 1000 jokes flashed round the world. For instance, what do you call a stockbroker in a restaurant? — Waiter!

(Sir Brian Wolfson, chairman, Wembley plc)

There is nothing like laughing at something scary to make it seem less daunting. Humour is not just a driving force in business, a tool or a weapon. It is also a coping device — a shield against failure, an antidote to boredom, a release for frustration and stress — each of which is experienced daily in organizations.

REASONS TO BE TEARFUL

Since business, like sport and war, is about winning and losing, there is a constant need for a force to attenuate defeat. That force is humour. Millionaire record producer Peter Waterman believes, 'If you're going to make millions, you've got to have a bit of humour; somewhere along the line you're going to be disappointed' (*Independent on Sunday*, 2 June 1991, p.75).

Humour helps us to confront failure in two ways: first, in our own minds, it puts failure into perspective; second, vis-à-vis others, it helps to smother accusations of incompetence.

Humour is a way of standing back from the immediate predicament or setback and taking a wider view. It serves as a reminder of the speed with which success turns sour, and a defence against the woes and vexations of business. Consider, for instance, the mechanical engineering firm which received three telephone calls of complaint in one week from disenchanted customers. The production manager's reaction: 'Well, look on the bright side. At least they're still talking to us.'

Humour helps us retain a sense of proportion, as demonstrated by the sales director who told his team, 'Last year we said, "things can't go on like this." And they didn't. They got worse.' Humour may not change the economic realities of failure, but it can help managers reframe misfortune in a more positive light. As Brian Pitman, chief executive of Lloyds Bank, explained, 'It is absolutely crucial to have a sense of humour, because it's the only thing that will keep you afloat when you hit the rocks. A sense of humour is vital to success' (Simcock, 1992, p.153).

The power of humour to transform painful or difficult situations is unparalleled. Humour feeds on failure. The proneness of managers to make mistakes and the regularity with which fate deals them duff hands are all grist to the mill.

Humour, then, cushions the impact of failure. Properly handled it can even turn setbacks to one's advantage. Managers who remain unflustered, who have the presence of mind to deflect misfortune with humour, may find their reputations enhanced, as in the early career of Sir Allen Sheppard:

I remember one of my first presentations to some of the directors at Ford where just about every damn thing that I was presenting came out wrongly. It was like a demonstration of Murphy's Law — the slides were in a different order from what I expected, at least a couple of them came out upside down. But I got away with it. Nobody realized, they all though it had been brilliantly rehearsed. They came up to me and asked me how long it had taken to prepare. I must admit I was a complete nervous wreck at the end of it, but it didn't show apparently. I managed to turn everything into a serious joke — to do with financial results! That was my first experience of using impromptu humour. From then on, I almost developed a reputation for it — and I had to live up to it. People used to come and ask me to do presentations.

Even with careful preparation, elaborate set-pieces, like presentations, are fraught with potential pitfalls: temperamental microphones, exploding lights and loud noises all conspire to interrupt proceedings. Although the precise nature of the mishaps is unpredictable, their likely intrusion is not. Managers should therefore be alert to the capacity of humour to transform threats into opportunities. Sheppard recalls:

> We began the Annual General Meeting with me asking the representative from the auditors to read out their audit on the accounts. I handed over to him but the microphone didn't work. This caused a great flurry as twelve people rushed up to the microphone. So I leant over to another mike and told the audience, 'You think that was an accident. In fact it was all rehearsed. They were going to qualify our accounts and I had to stop them somehow.' From that inauspicious start, the audience decided they were going to enjoy the AGM. And while the laughter settled down we managed to get the mike to work.

Granted, the line was not hysterical, but it was spontaneous and pertinent. The ensuing laughter is partly a mark of appreciation for improvised wit and poise. One of the advantages of using humour in the business setting is that it tends not to be expected. The threshold at which people are prepared to laugh is far lower than it would be, say, for a stand-up comic.

What is more, the build-up of tension in difficult circumstances often predisposes the audience to laughter. Take the example of a manager presenting a commemorative gift to his departing female deputy. As she walked forward to accept it, she stumbled and fell. There was a moment of concerned silence and embarrassment until the boss helped her up and said, 'Don't worry, women are always falling at my feet.'

His quip served as a lightning-rod for the collective anxiety. It confirmed that she was not hurt, as well as diverting attention from her loss of dignity and onto his resourcefulness.

Or again, consider the experience of Sir Brian Wolfson:

> Just as I was about to introduce the plenary speaker, I was handed a message saying he was running 20 minutes late. I looked at this and went absolutely silent. Then, I looked up at the expectant audience and said,

'Well, we have two alternatives: either I can go straight into the closing speech or you can listen to me ad lib for twenty minutes.'

By making light of the situation, Wolfson demonstrated his ability to take the unexpected in his stride and immediately put the audience at ease. This is vital if the audience is to remain receptive. Presenters who choose to ignore awkward incidents are likely to convey an impression of nervousness or inattention. This will leave the audience feeling uncomfortable and distracted. Either way, they will cease to concentrate on the contents of the presentation. A humorous acknowledgement rapidly dissipates audience tension and shows robustness.

This use of humour to extricate oneself from difficult situations also applies to mishaps of one's own making. By getting their jokes in early, managers can stifle allegations of failure or incompetence.

GAGGING THE OPPOSITION

Humour often serves to defuse the criticism levelled at us by others. It has become something of a cliché among comedians that they honed their comic talent from an early age as a way of not getting beaten up at school. They have their corporate equivalents. As Sir Allen Sheppard explained:

Going back into the dim and distant past, I guess that humour was linked in part to a lack of self-confidence. One way of heading off any criticism of yourself is to laugh at yourself before anyone else can.

Sheppard recalls digressing from a presentation to try to explain the background to an ongoing argument in the brewing industry. Realizing that he was straying somewhat from the original point, he checked himself and slipped in an aside, 'the actual debate is shorter than my summary'. Just as his audience might have been starting to think 'he's rambling on a bit', Sheppard himself voiced the unhatched criticism thereby lancing it.

When we dig a hole for ourselves, humour is on hand to give a leg-up. Having made a mistake, the trick is to make a joke of it before others can. As Sir Brian Wolfson put it, 'Self-deprecation goes down rather well in Britain – people will always join in if you invite them to laugh at you, with you.'

Humour disarms aggressors. By pre-empting the laughter of others, we steal their thunder. It isn't possible to sneer at the indolent administrative manager who claims that he rents piles of paper to put on his desk and make himself look busy. Nor can we further deride the veteran salesman who boasts that he has 'had more liquid lunches than you've had hot dinners'. Accusations of fecklessness or stupidity lose their punch if the accused has already voiced them. In the classic play, *Cyrano de Bergerac*, the hero ridicules himself with such wit that it is his aggressor who is left looking foolish.

A FIG LEAF FOR PERSONAL FAILINGS

"Why not admit it, Henry – you don't like people to notice you're scared."

WAY-OUT HUMOUR

Humour can also serve as an escape hatch, as Sara Webb found out when reporting for the *Financial Times* on how women fared in the City:

> At lunch with a group of futures and options traders, the traders were asked how many women were employed by the company, one of them piped up 'well there's X – he's pretty effeminate' whereupon they all collapsed laughing.

(*Career Choice Supplement*, 1991–2, p.9)

A similiar line in evasive tactics was sometimes employed by Henry Kissinger:

Kissinger camouflaged his defensiveness about his knowledge of international economics – or lack of it – with humour. He concluded a news conference in Vladivostok following the Ford–Brezhnev meeting by replying to a reporter, 'I didn't hear the question, but it dealt with economics so I don't want to answer it.'

(Valeriani, 1979, p.28)

Fielding tricky questions in this way is risky. Unless it is followed by a serious response, the questioner will feel the interviewee is being dismissive. The fact remains that a jokey response can, at least, lighten the mood and buy sufficient time to come up with a plausible answer. Thus, managers who have to speak on behalf of their company should build up a repertoire of throw-away lines to help them handle awkward questions.

A humorous response can also take the sting out of a hostile audience. Managers who respond aggressively to antagonistic questions may find the conflict escalating. Humour helps to halt the negative momentum and regain control of a charged situation. It recaptures audience attention and puts them in a more neutral and receptive frame of mind.

Even in the worst scenario, where the company does not wish to make a public statement, humour can still be used to keep relations sweet. When hounded by journalists, a response like, 'It's against my religion to talk to the press' (anon, *Sunday Times*, 26 January 1992, p.1) will probably go down better than an unimaginative 'No comment' – on top of which levity generally conveys optimism.

Or again, when called upon to refute an allegation, humour is sometimes a better option than a straight denial. For instance, a report in the *Daily Express* gossip column claimed that Lords Hanson and King had fallen out over British Airways' decision to cancel all advertising, which would prove detrimental to Hanson's fledgling, Melody Radio Station. The reported rift was erroneous, but how to dispel rumours without fuelling speculation? *The Times* revealed:

Since the men are close friends they regularly fax jokey messages, newspaper cuttings and cartoons to each other. Hanson, permitting a

rare moment of public insight into his sense of humour, wrote: 'Not only
are we still good friends, we are also deeply in love.'

(City Diary, 22 February 1991)

Humour also serves as an escape hatch when one person's serious
comment is treated like a joke. No matter how counterfeit it sounds,
laughter can provide a way out from the most awkward of
situations. It is not uncommon for employees to have requests
turned down in this way. When all else fails, when there seems no
logical defence to put forward, laughter is often the answer. It is
both unexpected and ambiguous. Those on the receiving end are
left feeling stupid and nonplussed, wondering if they have missed
something. As advertising agency chairman Winston Fletcher
wrote:

If you have failed to produce a promised document; if you have
bungled some simple arithmetic; if you are asked an embarrasing
question: laugh. If you treat the matter as an uproarious joke then, as
often as not your antagonist will fold his tent and pretend he was kidding
(though he was not). Laughter can be a devastating defensive weapon.

(Fletcher, 1983, p.160)

David Lodge also alludes to this means of self-defence in his novel,
Nice Work, with the reaction of a worldly secretary to her boss's
censure: '"Oh, you," said Shirley roguishly, adept at receiving
reprimands as if they were jokes' (Lodge, 1989, p.36).

It is not only other people's bullets that can be dodged in this
way. Humour can also serve to cover up a comment, serious or
otherwise, which has clearly misfired. For instance, the boss of a
manager who was being shadowed commented that the manager in
question was putting on a fine show: 'Trying to squeeze five days'
work into one, Steve?' The joke did not go down too well, so the
boss added 'As you always do, Steve.'

Another example was that of a middle management team trying
to persuade their boss to give more structure to his weekly
meetings. As it was, he operated a round robin system whereby the
time slots for each participant would become progressively shorter
as they edged towards lunchtime. They half-jokingly suggested
using a chess timer to limit contributions. The boss was clearly
taken aback by the implication that he lacked control over
meetings, so one of the managers jumped in to smooth his ruffled

feathers: 'We've found it very useful in our own meetings together to wake Tony up.'

Even serious comments which hit the wrong note can sometimes be retracted by passing them off as jokes. Thus someone who has caused offence may try to retrieve the situation by claiming that he or she is falsely accused of serious intent. One manager who upset a colleague by mentioning the fact that he was monopolizing a meeting room was able to claim retrospectively that his colleague had 'taken the bait' thus making his colleague look foolish for failing to recognize a 'wind-up.'

Besides helping managers to handle failure and failed initiatives, humour also allows them to live with anxiety and stress.

COPING WITH LABOUR PAINS

It is said that we laugh at funny stories because the punch line represents a release from the tension of the joke build-up. The person hearing the joke therefore receives a pleasurable stimulus. This is why we can become impatient with a person who tells a joke slowly or badly. In our anxiety to get to the tension release point we may even try to speed-up the story telling – so the longer the joke, the funnier it had better be. The same idea of release from stress makes humour an important mechanism in organizations.

SUPPRESSED HYSTERIA

"*You have nothing to reproach yourself for, Granville. Bigger men, stronger men, have giggled in board meetings.*"

Organizations are demanding places. They have an insatiable appetite for efficiency, improvement and logic. These challenges have intrinsic intellectual appeal but can become oppressive if there is no respite. The pressure, then, of maintaining a constant facade of rationality and responsibility can become too much. As Anthea Ballam saw it:

> The more serious and the more po-faced the profession, the greater the release has to be. It's like being in school assembly and being told something funny or singing the wrong words. You're in a situation where you're really not supposed to giggle, but you can't help it and I think that business is a bit like that.

She went on to explain how humour had sustained her through hard times:

> Five years ago we had a very bad year. We'd both been working separately as consultants and we formed a business partnership. When we moved into our new offices, we lost a lot of work which had previously been sub-contracted to us by big PR agencies, simply because we started trading under our own names. And the phone just stopped ringing. So we used to pick up the phone and talk into it for hours — or say 'for God's sake stop ringing' and slam the receiver down.

This use of humour as a psychological release, is also exemplified by Lord Carrington:

> When his secretary tells him that yet another television crew wants to interview him, he might say, 'Tell them to go and jump in the lake,' before agreeing to give them five minutes.
>
> (*The Times,* 9 November 1991)

However much they may enjoy their jobs, people cannot live their lives at a constant musical pitch of top C. Humour represents time-out from the strait-jacket of logic and responsibility. It briefly enables managers to disengage from their organizational roles.

This 'opt-out' facility is vital because it introduces the element of choice. It gives people back a measure of control which the organization has taken away from them. Confronted with a difficult situation, managers can choose to see the absurdity in it. This perception of enhanced control over one's work should not be underestimated: being able to laugh at a problem is the first step towards overcoming it.

Consider the case of two middle managers invited by their boss's boss to visit head office to take part in an informal chat. The junior of the two anxiously asked his more experienced colleague whether they needed to prepare in any way. 'Just stick a book down the back of your trousers', was the suggestion.

Humour can help us regain our sense of perspective in a way, or at least with a speed, that rational thought cannot. Humour does not just signal the start of recovery, but actually jump-starts it. For instance, a virus has just contaminated three days of work on the computer. The natural reaction is one of anger and frustration which is likely to impinge on the rest of the day's work. A vicious circle ensues whereby we become angry with ourselves for being irritable and frustrated at our continued inefficiency. To break out of this cycle by sheer willpower is not easy. We are too close to the action. Yet a burst of humour can lift us out of that situation. A problem which seems liable to overwhelm us can be reduced to its rightful proportions with a timely reminder, say, that 'We're all worm food in the end'. As one hotel general manager explained:

Above everything else you need a sense of humour — mainly because of the frustration. You have to be able to switch your mind to something else and forget the frustration. Humour helps you to put things behind you, to worry about the present, not the past.

Humour helps us to redraw our mental picture and to adopt a frame of mind that makes it possible to proceed. It allows us to liberate our minds from significance, to leave behind the 'It's-only-creative-if-it-sells' ethos of business, and to indulge our thoughts for the sheer gratification of the presnt. Humour is the intellectual version of 'playing truant'; it laughs jubilantly at what is forbidden both by reason and the responsibilities of employment.

Without this occasional reprieve, work becomes very stressful. As Sir Allen Sheppard explained, 'We try to have a relaxed management style, for the simple reason that we work our people terribly hard, so we'd have a pretty high nervous failure rate if we didn't allow them to relax.'

Humour, then, affords an escape from the boring or painstaking aspects of our work. Even when there is not a lot going on to get excited about, humour feeds our imagination and inventiveness. It keeps boredom and depression at bay.

Humour helps to dispel the sense of confinement, to rekindle enthusiasm and to make our working lives more like our social lives. It lets individuals express other aspects of their lives than work, other facets of their personality than the purely rational.

This, too, reduces tension. Since humour plays an important part in our social lives, introducing it into the workplace 'normalizes' the organization and helps us adjust to it. Take the example of a manager enquiring first thing in the morning whether a colleague has arrived:

Manager: 'Is he in yet?'

Colleague's secretary: 'He was but he's just popped out.'

Manager: 'He can't be down the pub already!'

In offices everywhere, such early morning exchanges help to ease the passage from domestic to work setting. By reducing the gap between life at work and life outside work we alleviate the tension, and enjoyable interaction with colleagues reduces the need for social support from outside the workplace. This theme is taken up by Sir Peter Parker:

The capacity to enjoy things in industry seems absolutely crucial because it enables people to think of their work as a real part of their lives, not something they feel constrained to do — and feel they've got to get away from.

This idea is echoed by Shandwick's Peter Gummer who heads the largest public relations group in the world:

You must have a sense of humour. If this all becomes too deadly serious, you end up being incredibly boring. You've really got to have a good time, otherwise, why the hell are we all doing it?

(Simcock, 1992, p.82)

So humour makes the work environment more varied and meaningful. It can be seen as a stabilizing force, a key to preserving managerial sanity.

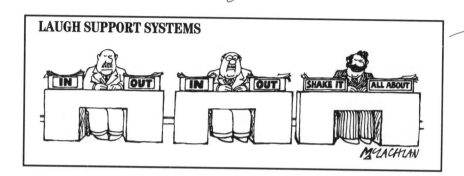

LAUGH SUPPORT SYSTEMS

MUDDLE MANAGEMENT

The intensity of organizational life is not the only thing which makes it stressful and calls for humour. Stress also arises from the collision between our abstracted view of business and the intricate reality. For instance, managers carry around a picture of an organizational chart in their heads, when what they actually experience is a complex web of interaction. To take another example, managers readily ascribe problems to particular departments – 'it's a marketing problem' or 'it's a production problem' – when in truth the problem invariably belongs to several departments at once. Our linear model of the world finds it difficult to handle mess.

The collision between reality and managerial interpretation is often most glaring when managers make presentations. Sir Allen Sheppard explains, 'When I'm giving a talk, I will generally interrupt myself with various side issues or comments, none of which are pre-planned.'

These 'comic asides' arise out of inconsistencies which pass unnoticed, say, when one is drafting a speech, or thinking up an excuse. They only materialize at the moment of delivery. One part of the brain ploughs the furrow it has rehearsed while the other part looks on in horror. Even as the vacuous assertion is uttered, the dissident voice inside is saying, 'You're never going to get away with this'. At this point, it is sometimes necessary to throw in a disclaimer of some sort to tone down triteness or inconsistency and salvage one's reputation.

The qualifying remark does not have to be especially witty. The combination of familiarity and surprise – the fact that it pin-points what others are thinking, while at the same time coming from an unexpected source – will be enough to raise a smile. It is just a case of giving voice to the running commentary of the interested cynic within. As Sir Peter Parker sees it, 'Humour is a bit like modern Christianity: it's all in you and the great thing is to release it.'

So, when inconsistency or paradox threaten to disrupt proceedings or undermine credibility, humour can be called upon. Humour keeps things flowing. It is perhaps in the routine ironing out of creases in the organizational fabric that humour makes its biggest contribution. Once humour is invoked, the idiosyncrasies of organizational life are transformed from a threat into a source of amusement, to be celebrated with others. Humour simultaneously acknowledges the irrationality and allows us to adjust to it by glorifying it.

Humour is a force in the direction of truth. It counters the tendency of the managerial mind to harbour faulty knowledge. Managers are constantly trying to make sense of data gleaned from diverse sources, and trying to make connections where none exist. The biggest problem for managers is not what they know but what they think they know. Through humour, managers grope towards the truth and incrementally purge their consciousness of these inferior insights. Managers, like scientists or mathematicians, are bent on discovering the true relations in a confusing and cluttered environment. In the words of Arthur Koestler, 'Comedy is paradox stated – scientific discovery is paradox resolved' (Koestler, 1964, p.95).

Take the scatological assertion of one manager that 'Meetings are like flatulence – you don't mind your own, but you can't stand anybody else's.' Indirectly, the observation confirms the experience of most managers: that of having to attend more meetings than they call, and the attendant frustration of not being in control of their time.

The analogy throws new light on one experience by likening it to another. Our minds gain insight through the comparison which nails down a deep-seated sentiment that has been privately drifting around the collective consciousness in a half-formed state. Again there is the joyous collision of surprise and familiarity which is vital to humour.

Or again, consider the boss who claims openness to feedback from his staff. The departmental wag warned colleagues: 'When he says he welcomes constructive criticism, he actually means praise.' Whether debunking work processes or summing up people, humour has an unerring ability to cut through appearances and get at the truth. As Arthur Koestler saw humour:

> It focuses attention on abuses and deformities in society of which, blunted by habit, we were no longer aware; it makes us suddenly discover the absurdity of the familiar and the familiarity of the absurd.
>
> (Koestler, 1964, p.73)

Those deformities are easily perpetuated in business. Executives' opinions are coloured by their ambitions. There is often a lack of boldness or plurality of vision which explains why committees can make collective decisions which their individual members would not dream of endorsing. Humour, according to *Director* editor Stuart Rock, is one way of breaking through that:

> Maybe it's an important constituent of any management team that you have someone who will argue the toss — not just a Devil's Advocate, or someone with a cynical, reductive view of life — but someone who can laugh at things all the time, and through comedy sees what the reality is — and can put things into perspective.

Perhaps there is a need to resurrect the role of court jester in latter-day companies; to nominate someone who has *carte blanche* to tell it like it is. The jester's role would not be to provoke change, it would simply be to help reconcile organizational myth and reality.

RITUALIZED REBELLION

Giving symbolic expression to the tensions that characterize organizational life is one way of lessening those strains. Within the realms of humour it is possible, say, to criticize the choices or competence of people on whom we depend (bosses, colleagues or customers). Humour is an outlet for the frustrations resulting from a sense of economic or organizational impotence.

Perhaps the most readily observable example of this token dissent can be seen in the offices of secretaries. Secretaries might frequently complain to peers about how they are put upon and mistreated, but they seldom remonstrate with the bosses themselves. When the boss needs a contract typed at 4.45 p.m. their expression may betray their exasperation, but it will tend to go unarticulated. Instead, they vent their discontent obliquely through assorted *bons mots*, cartoons and parodied letters which festoon their offices. Typically, these take as their target the boss's absentmindedness and lack of common sense or consideration. The following piece gives a flavour of the criticism:

TEN COMMANDMENTS FOR DICTATORS

1. Always begin dictation at 12 noon and 5.00 p.m. Mark your work 'URGENT' and then go home. Typists have no home.

2. When dictating, speak as indistinctly as possible. It develops the mastoid cells of the typist. Smoking or putting your hand over your mouth aids pronunciation and removes wrinkles. Speaking while yawning entertains the typist no end.

3. Always wait until the typist comes into the room before sorting out papers, seeking the references, receiving callers, and telephoning. Typists have plenty of spare time and urgent work is rare.

4. Ensure that important details, like names of people and places, are given at fast speeds and under no circumstances spell them. Typists know everybody, everywhere.

5. If the typist has the audacity to ask you to repeat a word, either:
   a) bawl at the top of your voice — intermittent deafness is an occupational disease with typists;
   b) babble and take no notice — typists enjoy a good game of 'Guess the missing word'.

6. If, after the work has been typed, you decide you dislike the wording, don't hesitate to alter it. Typists love doing work over again for they are natural perfectionists.

7. If enclosures are missing out of correspondence, blame the typist. Her memory is infallible and she understands every detail of everybody's letters.

8. After dictating for an hour, wait ten minutes then send for the typist and ask her for your work. It is sure to be done. Never say 'Please' or 'Thank you' – it brings on asthma.

9. Always pause for several minutes between each burst of dictation. Typists have a powerful dramatic instinct and delight in intense moments of silence.

10. When the facts of your letter depend upon information possessed by several other people in the office, send the typist round the building to collect it. Typists revel in a giddy whirl of social calls. When you come to those parts of your dictation where you don't know the names, etc., keep repeating 'you can dig that up later'. Typists become imbued with gratitude for constant reminders of things they cannot forget.

This represents a sort of open letter to bosses. Although they have not actually composed it, the secretaries endorse the sentiment by giving the document a prominent position in the office where their bosses are bound to see it. Why, then, does this not present a real challenge to authority? Surely the fact that the boss will see it means that he or she may take the criticism on board. Perhaps. The point is that this is all done with the blessing of the boss.

In tolerating such jokes, those in authority are effectively affirming the power which the secretaries pretend to deny. The fact that 'subversive' humour is allowed and even encouraged (through open laughter) implies that the social institutions and the people in power are strong enough to tolerate it; the rebellion turns into a twisted form of loyalty, a negative homage.

Giving vent to criticism through humour allows the person criticized to take the comment at face value and ignore any serious intent, however thinly veiled. The ambiguous nature of humour does not just reduce resistance; it also reduces potential compliance. Take the construction manager visiting one of the site managers who reports to him. The boss rounds off their meeting with an open-ended comment, 'Is there anything else you need from me?' Grasping the opportunity, the site manager starts to reel off a list, 'pay rise, new car, promotion . . .' Rather than address the matter head-on, his boss chooses to reply in kind: 'Sure, you'll get them next week, or can you wait 'till the week after?' The mechanism which allows jokers to take risks also prevents them from being fully effective as change agents. It is a matter of deciding who responds best to what means of persuasion.

A final source of stress in organizations is uncertainty – and that is primarily associated with the prospect or the fact of change.

THE BIG C

People tend not to like change. It induces stress, irrespective of its direction: whether it is change for the better or for the worse. As a result, people make up little routines and stick to them: from which side of the bed they sleep on or which armchair they use to what they eat for breakfast and what order they eat it in.

Work is no different. Managers have daily and weekly meetings; they base plans on the assumption that what has worked well in the past will work well in the future; they establish budgets in relation to last year's sales, not anticipated sales; and they persist with procedures that no longer make commercial sense. Beneath all the managerial rhetoric about embracing change, about change being 'the only constant in this organization', there is an ingrained fear of change.

At its coarsest, humour is used to scupper any movement which might entail change. Innovative suggestions invariably have a weakness – if only that they diverge from what has gone before – and an incisive one-liner is often enough to draw attention to it. As Sir Allen Sheppard explained:

> You can let people build their case right up and then go bang, and destroy the whole edifice. And the person you've just deflated will still speak to you at the end of it because it was 'only a joke'.

It is a fact of psychological life that people process and accept negative information more easily than positive information. The idea of spiking a whole line of argument or wave of enthusiasm with an appropriate cynicism is also exposed, tongue in cheek, by William Davis:

Ridicule is a powerful weapon. If a rival comes up with a really good idea — one which may win him promotion — you can undermine his self-confidence (and raise doubts in the minds of others) by treating it as a joke. Smile and say: 'You are not really serious about this, are you?' If he persists, home in on the weakest aspect of his case (there is always one) and make fun of it. If two or three others join in the laughter the good idea is dead.

(Davis, 1984, p.34)

If no obvious weakness springs to mind, it is possible to undermine the credibility of the speaker with a joke like, 'What's it like on the planet where you live?' Again, cheap but effective.

Of course, humour is not just used destructively as a means of maintaining the status quo. It will also serve to ventilate the feelings of anxiety and stress surrounding the prospect of change. Take the example of a manager in an insurance company which was in a state of 'structural flux.' Asked what his current priorities were, he answered, 'Checking the office door every morning, to see that my name's still on it.' By exaggerating the source of his anxiety, the threat was made to seem more remote and less daunting.

Or again, consider the restructuring of the New Zealand health sector. In order to minimize disruption to the system, the government announced that 99 per cent of staff would transfer automatically to the new organization. Only the senior managers would be made to reapply for their jobs. Prior to the next senior management meeting, one of the participants put up the printed sign, 'Welcome to the one per cent club!' Humour, then, distances those enduring relentless change from their circumstances. It keeps them flexible and upbeat.

From the point of view of those initiating change, humour conveys a sense that things are going to be all right, that the changes can be managed. It suggests faith in the future without having to resort to heavy-handed propaganda. A speech to the City by the Chancellor of the Exchequer saying, 'Don't Panic!' is almost guaranteed to send sterling plummeting. The reason for this is that 'Don't Panic!' is not a message but a stimulus. 'I'll sell every pound I've got before the market closes' is a possible response.

Similarly, in the organizational context, a solemn statement that there is nothing to worry about is bound to raise suspicion. On the other hand, a light-hearted approach communicates confidence in a subliminal way. For instance, a managing director is asked whether a troublesome project has picked up at all. He answers, 'At this rate, we're going to have to drill a hole in the floor just to keep track of our profit curve.'

Ironically, this serves to dissipate the fear surrounding the future of the project, the reasoning being that if things were really so bleak he would not joke like that. Similarly, a comment like 'We're in it deeper than dung beetles' helps to take the edge off a serious predicament. It is taken as a sign that the problems can be handled. If, in spite of the pressure, the leader can smile it can have a real impact on morale, for people tend to take their cue from their leaders.

The same goes for public announcements by chairmen. With the impending electricity privatization lurching from one setback to another, Norweb chairman Ken Harvey seemed hassled and worried. However, when asked how he was coping with the stress of leading a public utility kicking and screaming into the private sector, he explained that he was 'sleeping like a baby – I fall asleep for ten minutes and then I wake up crying' (*The Times*, City Diary, 15 August 1990). Again, the capacity to joke often conveys a positive outlook more effectively than some emphatic proclamation.

Finally, it is worth looking at a phenomenon which encompasses a number of the themes already discussed, including failure, anxiety, and ritualized rebellion. It concerns the popular appeal of humorous business books.

IN SEARCH OF IRREVERENCE

The first humorous book about management to make its mark was *Parkinson's Law* by the late C. Northcote Parkinson, which opened with the famous assertion that 'Work expands so as to fill the time available for its completion' (Parkinson, 1958, p.4). The book quickly achieved bestseller status, and the approach attracted other authors. By the early 1970s there was already a substantial body of light-hearted literature on business, ranging from *The Peter Principle* by Laurence Peter and Raymond Hull to *Up the Organization* by Robert Townsend.

These books were different from previous management fare – academically inclined offerings such as Peter Drucker's *The Practice of Management* (1955) – insofar as they were readable, diverting and punchy. Yet they differed not just in style but also in perspective. Where business books had conventionally focused on administrative dynamics, humorous books have always been concerned with people and the way people 'make out' in organizations.

Their authors hand out gustily unconventional advice to those who really want to negotiate the three-piece jungle, the dominant theme being that upward mobility has little to do with hard work or merit and that those who succeed are merely the ones who are the best at getting promoted. The writing is suffused with amoral, jocular cynicism. Methods of achieving success are evaluated by the simple *realpolitik* criterion: do they work? There is no pretence that anyone is interested in efficiency, fairness or the achievement of the firm's goals for their own sake. Corporations are portrayed as important for the sole reason that they represent peaks for ambitious young managers to scale.

These humorous books on corporate skulduggery now form an established strand of the mainstream management literature. No Christmas book list is complete without a sprinkling of corporate survival guides and tactical handbooks telling readers how to dupe recruiters, how to discredit rivals and how to manage their bosses.

These books would not be funny if they were not based on truths, but does that make them realistic? Does the fact that they lay bare rampant self-interest make them useful tactical guides? Winston Fletcher, author of *Meetings, Meetings*, thinks not:

I don't think anyone would do any of these things neat, but it makes you slightly more conscious of what goes on in meetings, so you are rather better at handling them. You look at them with a fresh eye — they become less intimidating and less boring.

(Conversation with author)

Taken literally, then, the career tips for thrusting young executives – along the lines 'how to get your boss's job' or where to position one's desk in order to inflict maximum psychological damage on colleagues – could seriously damage their careers. This would suggest that the real value of these books lies elsewhere: perhaps in the vicarious thrill we derive from the *thought* of screwing the company. This sort of writing suggests an implausible level of control over our corporate destinies, but it is still useful in helping to persuade us that organizations are not such hard-to-manage places.

The complex workings of the organization are reduced to the level of a child's game. Using humour, this literature helps us to come to terms with the confusion we experience daily. Humour enables us to see some of the ambiguities and contradictions of organizational life which our rational model of the world finds it difficult to accommodate. So for those whose real attitude to their workplace is a mixture of boredom and apprehension, these success and autonomy fantasies help them adjust. They make the corporation seem banal. That which is made matter-of-fact is not daunting: that which is entertaining can be lived with.

There is also a case for saying that these humorous books serve as an antidote to executive alienation. Their emergence in the 1960s perhaps marked the realization that executive life may well be exciting for those who are successful, powerful, or who benefit from real opportunities to exercise their creative talents. But how many executives really enjoy this kind of stimulation? If the majority do not, but feel that their outlets and opportunities are narrowed and that satisfactions are more extrinsic – material rewards, security, status – then this literature can be seen as escapist. These are bibles for the bypassed, just as Mills and Boon

DIMINISHED RESPONSIBILITY

"Stop moaning, Mason . . . Lots of people would give their right arm to be a paper-weight."

offer succour to those whose lives lack romance. They are a means of escape from a reality that is both unattainable and unsatisfying at the same time.

Also, by representing people who reach the top as hard-nosed thugs and hatchet men, these books offer implicit consolation to those who feel harried or inadequate and find themselves languishing in the organizational backwaters. If we can laugh at the antics of the hyper-ambitious we can cope with not being like them. The thought that others have kicked, licked and hacked their way to the top gives those at the bottom a sense of moral superiority. It helps allay any pangs of failure among those who got off the fast track or were never able to get on to it. They can righteously pat themselves on the back for not stooping to these tricks and for adopting a more balanced approach to life. They may even justify their underachievement by suggesting that the career-obsessed are merely compensating for personal problems, low self-esteem, dissatisfaction or failure in *real life*.

Teeming with 5 Humour

I think the skilful manipulation of atmosphere — because it is manipulation to some extent — is what creates an atmosphere for people to give of their best, for people to feel good about themselves, for people to feel comfortable and warm. Laughing together is among the most agreeable and binding of human activities.

(Sir Brian Wolfson, Chairman, Wembley plc)

Humour is not just of value to individuals. It is also important to groups as a means of establishing and perpetuating shared values, as a kind of social cement. Far from being a superficial froth on social relationships, humour is central to any collective endeavour.

It was established earlier that humour is situation specific. What is funny in one setting won't be in another. But beyond that, the comic worth of an event or remark depends on the group viewing it. Humour is in the eye of the beholder.

For instance, within a company, the idea of a salesman having to drive a Lada from the company car pool as punishment for careless driving is likely to tickle people in sales more than those in accounts or on the shop-floor. Similarly, those in the production department will derive more malicious pleasure from hearing of a marketing foul-up than the people, say, in personnel. And a broken lift is more likely to be a source of amusement for those on the ground floor than anyone else.

Humour is intimately tied to group culture. What makes a group laugh provides an insight into common values and perspectives –

from the smallest gathering of three people right through to UK plc and beyond.

THREE'S A CLIQUE

A column in *The Times Educational Supplement* started:

> The other day at an anniversary party, I was feeling uncomfortably distant from two once close friends of 15 years ago, when one said, 'Sue and I reached a new climax of sexual union last Saturday night.' My alarm rose for a split second as he continued. 'We both had a headache together.'
>
> (*TES*, 24 April 1987, p.21)

A somewhat awkward situation was immediately relieved and a previous bond reinstated by shared laughter. The intimacy which would have taken some time to achieve through formal interaction was achieved instantly with humour – in much the same way as reminders of old nicknames and funny stories can provide short cuts to renewed acquaintance.

The very smallest group protects itself against outsiders and gives itself identity using humour. Indeed, it could be said that a group's independent existence is marked by the creation of its own jokes, jesters and scapegoats. In some offices, for instance, the name of an unpopular individual is turned into a verb and secretly used to designate a form of behaviour associated with that person. One example encountered was 'Thorped', which served as short-hand for 'to be trapped in lengthy conversation', as in 'I've just been Thorped.'

Running jokes like these are the exclusive property of the in-group. They strike implicit chords and seal a clique. Past failures, close shaves or fluky successes become so much fuel for groups to draw on once the negative side of the event is dulled by time. And the generation of future jokes from present hardships is confirmed by the cliché, 'We'll laugh about it some day'. Shared experiences and setbacks become the building blocks of group solidarity.

Often, these incidents actually rely on the group for their definition as humour. To the office newcomer, 'the funniest thing that ever happened', narrated several times at great length, has the entertainment value of someone reading out the telephone directory. Fortunately, the qualification 'you had to be there' will be

A VITAL MEMBER OF THE TEAM

SMART HARD WORKING OFFICE HAS VACANCY FOR A FAT SLOB REQUIRED TO BE THE BUTT OF JOKES

proffered to excuse outsiders for their failure to laugh while those around them fall about.

This kind of humour is arguably the least amusing, yet the most powerful in the workplace. It derives its funniness from the specific relationship between the people who were there at the time. It is meaningful only to them. It creates a sense of community.

GAGGED AND BOUND

The late Frankie Howerd once said that people tend to cry at the same things, but laugh at different things. Sometimes the same people laugh at different things at different times. That was the perspective of a stand-up comedian. It is not so where groups are concerned. Within groups the prime function of humour is to bind, not necessarily to amuse or divert.

People need to feel they are accepted members of the groups to which they belong and shared laughter is an effective way of satisfying that need. We feel pleased when others laugh at our jokes. More than applauding our wit, they are confirming our group membership. And by laughing at their jokes (however weak) we affirm our status as insiders. Not to laugh is to risk ostracism.

The use of humour to generate group laughter is also a means of bringing people into line. Humour can be directed at someone in the group who either has not learned or has violated the norms of the group. For instance, one manager arrived late to a brainstorming session with some of his peers. The leader of the session commented, 'You realize we're going to have to punish you for this?' Another manager added enthusiastically, 'And I'll be the one to administer it.' There was no need for resentment or self-justification on the part of the wrongdoer. The only response expected of him was laughter. He obliged, thereby acknowledging the offence and symbolically pledging renewed allegiance to the group. Cohesion was maintained and correction achieved without confrontation or loss of face.

Collective laughter reinforces the veiled criticism and makes the transgressor more likely to accept the criticism. As one departmental manager explained, 'The mere presence of others adds weight to teasing or censure and helps you to "round up the strays".'

Of course, bonding is not only achieved by directing humour internally. Group norms will also be reinforced by mocking external targets.

THE PLEASURE OF HATING

Humour also expresses the group's shared resistance to the social pressures and tensions of the outside world. Much group joking directs itself against the rottenness of everything outside the group's boundaries. A group will reinforce its own identity or values by routinely disparaging other groups, particularly those with which it is in competition or on which it is dependent.

Typically, this denigration focuses on the poor grasp on reality of those above. For instance, workers will joke about the management trainee 'with a book and a degree who doesn't know the difference between 99.9 and 100'. The workers may joke about common practices which are either unsafe or prohibited – and which would horrify management – but which allow them to do their work more easily. They may joke about these practices, or deride management's obliviousness to them. Norman Augustine relates the instance of one veteran worker confiding to a student beginning a summer job in a large factory: 'If you really want to mess up the company, do exactly what they tell you' (Augustine, 1986, p.337). Such joking helps to perpetuate the worker's 'common-sense' view of their work while at the same time reinforcing group norms, and such behaviour is not confined to bolshie workers. Secretaries will heap scorn on the handwriting, poor spelling or hideous syntax of those who give them work, not to mention their bosses' lack of organization or consideration. In doing so, secretaries are also redefining their own status from a position of subservience to one of authority – a sort of quality control function.

Nor are managers immune from making snide asides about their seniors. One middle manager when referring to the level above sarcastically remarked, 'Sometimes we actually *get things done* – if they leave us alone.' And there is widespread disdain for the remoteness of those at board level. Fun is poked at the board members whose only targets are the holes on the local golf course and whose idea of long-range planning is to decide where to go for lunch. In subsidiaries everywhere, what goes on at corporate headquarters, known in some companies as 'The Kremlin' and in others as 'The Bunker', is remorselessly belittled.

Directors from head office are often given funny nicknames to make them seem less intimidating or to forewarn newcomers. For instance, one thrusting young marketing director was dubbed 'the flip chart kid', an exacting personnel director was known to her staff as 'Atilla the Hen', an inept autocrat was rechristened 'Genghis Can't', and a less-than-candid director in a British construction company earned the sobriquet 'the smiling assassin'.

Directors may even be given a collective name. In the British subsidiary of one American firm the people at the American head office were known as 'The Septics' (rhyming slang for Yanks). At ITT they are known as 'seagulls' because, as one long-suffering manager explained, 'they fly in, make a loud noise, eat your food, shit on everyody and fly out again.' And in a national newspaper group the directors were dubbed 'the lunch bunch'. Cocking a snook at those on whom we depend is a way of making our lives more bearable. It helps us to maintain a sense of detachment and to cope when we incur their displeasure.

What is more surprising perhaps is that the head of the subsidiary will often condone, not to say encourage, this contempt for head office personnel. One plant manager joked with his juniors about the presentation skills of the group finance director, giving him the make-believe billing: 'Dave Woodward and his amazing soporific

THEM AND US

UNITED AMALGAMATIONS LTD

BOARD ROOM

"Do you think the directors ever pretend to be us?"

voice'. This prompted a run of jokes about the group finance director, the gist of which was that his Brummie accent, cunningly allied to a nasal drawl, made listening to him for periods of more than five minutes inconceivable. Such joking provides a focus around which to rally members of the management team in the subsidiary.

Joking about the ineptitude of those above is a way of bringing them down to our level. For instance, jokes about officers are most poignant for sergeants, not privates. And in organizations, even the directors may allow themselves a wry smile when they see their omniscient chairman drop everything in order to tend the needs of a government official. It is funny because the directors are not used to seeing their boss shorn of his grandeur. 'You can tell that the minister's coming, 'cos the boss is wearing his knee pads,' said one director. 'And a condom on his tongue,' capped another.

It is perhaps to alleviate our collective anxiety and self-doubt that we project qualities of stupidity and incompetence on to those who have risen above us in the hierarchy. The jokes undermine the legitimacy of their success by ascribing to those people the trait of ineptitude, the hallmark of failure in the business context.

People like to think they have risen to the hierarchical level that they have *chosen* to occupy – as opposed to the highest level they were *capable* of attaining. If managers thought that everything were decided on effort, excellence and expertise, then life would be pretty difficult to bear for those not promoted. It is more comforting to believe in the unfairness of life: 'My face just doesn't fit.'

Individuals therefore draw comfort from exposing the inadequacies of those above them in the organization. It confirms that seniors got to where they are on something other than merit, luck being the most charitable explanation. So, every time we joke about the competence of others, we are questioning their right to be there, their credentials, their worthiness. There is a delicious pleasure in briefly glimpsing the frailties, vanities and perversities of those in charge: catching one's boss in mid-putting action, or hastily concealing a pocket mirror, or even a slip of paper filled with practised signatures. Finding humorous failings in others provides consolation for those whose careers plod along to the beat of a different drum – for if we cannot see these weaknesses in our seniors, then the weaknesses must be in us.

Of course, differentiation in companies is not just a top-down affair. Organizations are not just layered in terms of authority, they are also differentiated by function – sales, finance, production, and so on. These departments need to be co-ordinated, and the shortfall between synchronized perfection and everyday confusion is a vast ocean of comic potential. Here again is the idea of tension as a wellspring of humour.

WHO HATES WHOM

The aim of business is to produce more, of better things, with less – less time, less money, less materials, less labour. There is never enough to go round. This naturally puts a strain on relations between departments. Further tension arises from the fact that departments are dependent on other functions, but some are more dependent than others. Humour provides a channel through which to express and work out some of these tensions without endangering the collaborative venture as a whole. It follows that the flashpoints of humour in organizations occur where inter-functional friction is keenest, with jokes serving to relieve tension and change minds.

A study by Lockyer and Jones gives a reflection of the skewed relations between departments. Samples of managers from finance, marketing, personnel and production were asked to classify their relation with a range of other functions as satisfactory or unsatisfactory.

The outcome of this research was that managers from finance and personnel were paragons of virtue – well-adjusted, tolerant characters with few grievances against colleagues in other departments. Hardly surprising perhaps, in view of the more detached and desk-bound nature of much of their work. The marketing managers were less happy with the state of the world. They harboured a grudge towards R & D, fuelled no doubt by the failure of researchers to generate consumer-pleasing products; towards finance which obstructs claims for travel and entertainment expenses; but most of all towards production, reflecting an irritation at the unwillingness of production to agree to sales-enhancing changes.

Not to be outdone, the production managers described every single relationship as unsatisfactory. In particular, whatever hostility emanated from sales and marketing was amply reciprocated. Conclusive proof, it would seem, that production managers are recruited from the most cantankerous 10 per cent of the labour force. But a little more delving reveals that production work is particularly complicated and vulnerable, in that it is marked by a large degree of dependency on others, most notably on marketing and sales. This conflict between sales and production is neither local nor personal: it is in the logic of the situation. Sir Brian Wolfson explains, 'Conflict is legitimate in business – production is *supposed* to fight with sales – and humour is a way of diffusing conflict and of turning away hostility.'

The tension in their relationship is enshrined in Henry Ford's production-driven concession that customers could have any colour Model T they liked, 'as long as it's black'. Production likes to restrict the production range for ease of manufacture. Sales, on the other hand, likes to offer a wide range of products to help achieve bigger and better orders.

This constant friction between representatives of sales and production over prices and lead times, modifications and 'specials' and the wisdom of programme changes translates into a high level of interdepartmental sparring, not to mention the use of humour in actually resolving these imponderables.

But there is more to interdepartmental conflict than the inherent conflict of interests. Different departments are populated by wildly different types of people. So, allied to the rational tensions between departments, there are clashes of personality which open up further seams of humour.

At one end of the scale, the people in finance are written off as bean-counting, anal-retentives. At the other end there are the sales people ('all mouth and trousers') who are said not to mind which way they are going as long as they are getting there fast. Two worlds, divided by an unbridgeable gap of envy and contempt.

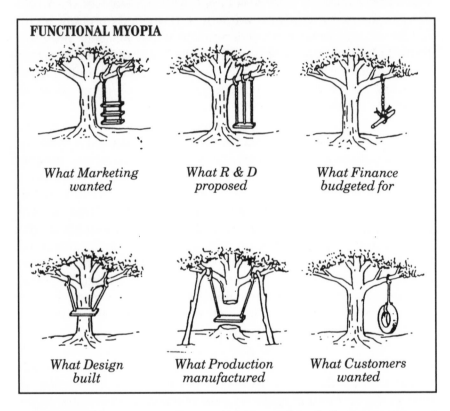

FUNCTIONAL MYOPIA

What Marketing wanted

What R & D proposed

What Finance budgeted for

What Design built

What Production manufactured

What Customers wanted

Caricatures these may be, but they are founded: the product of selection and socialization. Take, for instance, production managers. Relative to, say, finance specialists, production managers are less qualified, less well paid and less ambitious. They will also tend to be more down-to-earth, partly because they have opted for a more physical and less glamorous function, and partly because they are in constant contact with workers rather than staff people and well-groomed secretaries. Production management work is more action-orientated. Unlike finance people, production managers walk around a lot, they are physically active. They operate in noisy, dirty places, and they, or at least their charges, are occasionally exposed to physical danger around the workplace, whereas the worst injury likely to befall a finance manager is a twinge of budget elbow. These differences in experience and outlook result in humorous stereotyping.

Different departments therefore have different perspectives. They use different types of humour and their targets are different. What people are or are not allowed to laugh at, and what they actually laugh at, reflects and shapes departmental identity, and makes humour a critical element in the socialization process.

While people in organizations are broadly tied in to the humour of their peer group or function, there remains an element of personal choice. People have some control over their network of contacts and humour again is an important determinant of lines of communication.

LAUGH LINES

Humour is vital in shaping the rhythms of work and the patterns of contact within the organization. When we get bored we seek engagement, we make social calls to neighbouring offices, and humour provides the focal point of contact.

A sense of humour acts as a magnet, drawing others to see us. For instance, when people line their office walls with humorous cartoons or epigrams, it sends out a message to others, as would exhibiting one's diplomas and certificates. Funny signs or posters project one's view of the world, and trigger certain assumptions about one's character and attitudes. They are like open invitations to kindred spirits. The humour generally hinges on annoying, inappropriate or time-wasting behaviour in the workplace. It encourages comment and banter and helps people connect. In short, it makes work more sociable.

Lower-level employees are not the only ones who seek the occasional diversion of contact and humour. It is simply more obvious with them because their jobs involve more routine and desk-bound elements and because they have quite narrowly prescribed lines of communication. To stray from these, therefore, attracts immediate attention. Managers also seek engagement, but they are fortunate in that their job is all about interaction. Forget the popular image of the manager making decisions in Olympian isolation. Managers actually spend very little of their time at their desks, either reading or writing. They spend the bulk of their time working directly with others in meetings, and discussions on the telephone or face-to-face. So it could be said that much of their work is camouflaged fun. As Ralf Dahrendorf, former head of the London School of Economics wrote:

> The equivalent of the tea break with directors or professional people is drinks before lunch; the advantage they have over tea-drinking workers is that the drinks are in fact followed by a luncheon as well. Whereas working people stretch their work so that it begins to look like leisure, managers and professional people constrain their leisure so that it has at least the appearance of work.
>
> (Dahrendorf, 1982, p.46)

Consider tours of the workplace as an example of this camouflaged fun. These provide managers with an opportunity to show their faces, to be intercepted, to gather impressions and to pass on information and instructions. The idea is to nip problems in the bud, to pick up danger signals before they manifest themselves in the written data which managers receive. Management guru Tom Peters even set his personal seal of approval on this technique by dubbing it 'Management by Walking About' (MBWA), thereby legitimizing the process for any manager who felt slightly guilty about indulging in it. MBWA is justified as an opportunistic way of compressing numerous activities into a short space of time.

But if we set aside what is actually achieved on these tours and focus instead on their style, they come across as rather interesting jaunts and pleasantly chatty affairs. In between greeting workers and colleagues there are bouts of verbal jousting, ribbing and gossiping, as well as the mutual exchange of concerns and 'hot information'. What is more, humour plays an important role in dictating the shape of the tour. Managers will tend to choose their ports of call according to people who are good value, with whom they can share a joke, rather than on the basis of impartial logic. As advertising agency chairman, Winston Fletcher put it, 'If to go to someone's office and have a chat is not a pleasure, then you tend not to do it, except when you absolutely have to.'

These tours are rarely indispensable. There are invariably other ways in which managers could carry out their work. For instance, some of the unstructured exchanges could probably be pre-empted with more regular formal meetings; some of the anomalies picked up by walking about could no doubt be gleaned from careful scanning of computer printouts; and some of the instructions issued orally could probably be communicated by electronic mail. But none of these alternatives seems so appealing as face-to-face encounters which hold the promise of humour. Managers prefer the repartee, the cut and thrust of informal interaction. They are driven by the basic need for contact and their preference for other humans as sources of information, support and inspiration.

The ensuing web of communication has little to do with the formal lines of the organization chart. It follows that humour has quite an influence on the circulation of unofficial information, either because people contact those with whom they share a sense of humour, or because the information itself is given a humorous twist. The carrier of this sort of information is the corporate grapevine, that repository for dramatic and humorous vignette alike.

THE FRUITS OF THE GRAPEVINE

The corporate grapevine is not only the medium of fun; it is also a fun medium. The misdeeds and improprieties of the office often loom larger than those outside work, and can be sufficiently addictive to remain of interest to individuals who have left the organization.

Exchanging unguarded talk about people and events and trading in unsubstantiated facts is one of the pleasures of working life. Gossip is the currency of groups. Those who can do, those who can't talk about them. Columnist Reggie Nadelson wrote:

> Gossip doesn't give you Aids. It doesn't want to live in your neighbourhood. It is lots of fun and very cheap. Best of all, those who commit the stuff of major gossip stand in as our monsters . . . We watch them act out our most lurid fantasies, and feel superior.
>
> (*Independent,* 27 August 1992, p.20)

Gossip provides subjects for conversation, during lunch-hours and tea-breaks about the work of a company, and so widens interest in the work. It leavens the dull routine. There is nothing better guaranteed to bring a twinkle to the eye and a smile to the lips than a furtive glance followed by the lead-in, 'You mustn't repeat this . . .'. Gossip adds a bit of drama, as well as comic relief, to working lives. It plays a vital social and psychological role, especially for those at some distance from the apex. As Simon Carr once wrote, 'A happy staff is a productive staff. And what makes them happy is malicious gossip' (*Punch*, 25 November 1988, p.19).

THE CAPERLESS OFFICE

"Know what I really miss? Office rumours."

Just about everyone indulges in gossip in some form or other. The high-minded may feign indifference or couch it in respectability, like Tom Peters' 'naïve listening', but essentially it is still gossip. We like hearing it and, even better, we like passing it on. To have the inside dope on a matter is to possess, however briefly, real power. Conversely, one's corporate credibility can be ruined by presenting as hot gossip news which has already broken.

Gossip, like humour, is a great corporate leveller. Everyone indulges and no one is spared. To discover a shortcoming in superiors is to reduce them to human proportions. Gossip is the revenge of the humble on the pompous and self-important. Gossip is a perfect opportunity for action without responsibility.

The fun and conspiratorial element is heightened by the fact that the grapevine finds its own configuration. People choose the colleagues to whom they wish to pass on libellous nuggets. The telling of gossip reveals a lot more about the relationship between those who repeat it than those who generated it in the first place.

It can be fascinating trying to retrace the path of a rumour. Confidential information can change hands unknowingly, in a casual aside. For instance, information on salary discrepancies may get passed on, sometimes even going outside the organization boundaries and involving partners or offspring, only to re-enter at some later stage. Sometimes the route is so tortuous that it cannot be reconstituted. At other times the rumour is just the result of an inspired piece of deduction. Thus a note read upside-down on a desk, or a snatch of conversation overheard in the washroom may be enough to set a rumour in motion. Similarly, a formal appointment with the head of personnel is bound to set tongues wagging.

The problem is that we like to see patterns in the world around us. As one hotel general manager saw it, 'You get different bits of information from different sources and sometimes you get a piece of the jigsaw which connects one side of the board to the other.'

The incomplete bits of data which managers exchange may mean little out of context to the uninitiated, but a great deal to someone who is well connected. An item of information gleaned from another source can fit so well into the puzzle of an interested party that it confirms or changes his or her course of action. Word-of-mouth communication has a strong impact and is convincing, so people are disposed to give credit to gossip which they imagine, rightly or wrongly, is untainted by vested interests.

Fax and electronic mail, Tannoy and newsletter, are left standing by the pace of any message wrapped in tittle-tattle. For instance, repeated attempts at one manufacturing plant to coax workers to respect safety procedures proved fruitless; managers set a self-conscious example by wearing hard hats on the shop-floor and making threatening noises to the effect that the boss had 'a bee in his bonnet about safety'. But all to no avail. Accident prevention is inherently uninteresting.

What did eventually drive home the message was the black humour surrounding an accident in which one of the lathe operators lopped off a digit. Jokes such as 'I've heard about giving management the finger, but this is ridiculous', inadvertently served to spread the safety message in a way that no 'engineered' campaign could have achieved. Humour sped up the circulation of the safety message by making it interest-grabbing and instantly retellable.

Or again, consider the story related by Hearn and Parkin of 'the "new lad . . . with Diplomas Galore" who came to the shop floor of an engineering factory and . . . had a french letter on his back by ten o'clock' (1987, p.126). The anecdote lends itself to exaggeration and further elaboration – and the way it is reshaped will say a lot about the prevailing view of authority, work, initiation, youth and education.

The point, then, is that the grapevine has a logic of its own. It picks up and spreads what it wants to hear: the unusual, the grotesque, the denunciatory, the salacious or the surprising. In many ways, the grapevine enshrines the collective memory of the organization. It is a far more authentic representation of the company than the sanitized material contained in annual reports, company newsletters and press releases.

ORGANIZATIONAL JOKELORE

The funny stories that float round a company provide an uncensored view of its inner workings and of its shared beliefs. It could even be said that organizations are defined by what goes on near their boundaries. All the scams and unauthorized activities which occur at the fringes help to determine what is, and what is not, possible within the company. Few of these practices or events are ever recorded officially. They are simply passed on by word of mouth, like the story of the brewery manager who was caught stealing four cans of beer and, rather than being sacked, was allowed to hand in a backdated letter of resignation. Such incidents provide more insight into the way a company conducts its business than any ethical policies document.

Among the more colourful stories encountered, there was the management team that gave putting pars to each of their offices; the staff who ran a sweepstake on how long the boss's new secretary would last; and the aggrieved insurance employee whose parting salvo on being dismissed was to reword the standard letter of condolence so that it read: 'The company extends its sincerest sympathy to you in your bereavement. Never mind, the money's on its way.' There was also the factory worker who requested, in his will, that his coffin be strapped to the top of an ice-cream van, complete with chirpy tune, and driven past the factory gates to give his workmates one last laugh. A sort of posthumous fly-past.

These episodes exist only in the oral medium. They are funny because they so obviously contravene organizational norms, but they also test out the elasticity of organizational boundaries and reinforce the way organizations see themselves. Stories are powerful communicators of the company's distinctive competence and philosophy. People are inclined to reason by means of tales, not policy manuals or mission statements. The actual accuracy of such events is not at issue. If an event appears real, then it is real in its effects.

Alongside the humorous incidents which may actually shape the corporate culture there are the more conventional jokes which tend to reflect it. A passing remark will often provide a pithy encapsulation of corporate mores. For instance, the ingrained conservatism of one British insurance company was mocked by managers who came up with a variation on the SAS slogan: 'Who dares, P45'. And the big joke at Big Blue is that IBM stands for 'I've Been Moved', focusing on the company's obsession with managerial mobility.

Of course, standard jokes move with the times and the dominant concerns. For instance, at the time when British Leyland was on the brink and the catch phrase 'everybody out' was all the rage, jokes such as 'The workers have taken to signing the visitors' book instead of clocking on' went round the company. Similarly, at Jaguar, when quality hit an all-time low in the mid-1970s, there was 'What's the difference between a Jag and Jehovah's witness? You can shut the door on a Jehovah's Witness.' Those jokes are no longer pertinent. New preoccupations have taken over.

Thus senior managers looking to make improvements might start by listening out for the sorts of jokes doing the rounds. Take the case of a highly-pressurized department in an oil company where a total of six people had recently suffered either strokes or heart attacks. The tell-tale jokes in that environment hinged on being paid by the burst blood vessel and organizing heart attack rotas.

Not all the jokes target the company itself. Corporate values are also reflected in the jokes directed at competitors, suppliers, clients and government. Much of the humour is ingrained, with executives mocking suppliers who cannot handle routine orders, or finding humour in the stupidity of customers. For instance, the head of department of an insurance company was asked by a young clerk whether the company could accept payment of premiums by Giro. The manager explained that it was not possible, adding dismissively, 'They'll be wanting to pay with livestock or coloured beads next.' Implicitly, remarks like these say a lot about the view that the company has of its policy-holders. It indicates whether the prevailing view is of the customer as king or clown.

Such jokes tell newcomers to the organization a great deal about how they are expected to view their work, their contribution, the company, its suppliers, its competitors and its customers.

MOCK EXAMINATION

The jokelore carries within it the assumptions and values that new employees should espouse. They will find that the jokes and stories provide accurate snapshots of what the company is really like. Gaining acceptance is about knowing whether the dominant ethos is 'don't rock the boat' or 'look busy'. And that can't be found in the rule book.

Newcomers will find these humorous sound-bites useful in other ways. Besides the information they contain, a lot can be inferred from the way they are passed around. Joking patterns serve as an impartial guide to the relative status of people in the newcomer's entourage. Certain group members will have hub roles in the humorous exchanges while others may barely partake.

A study by Duncan and Feisal (1989) identified two types of managers who were pretty much excluded from the flows of banter in the groups they managed. They dubbed these the arrogant executive and the benign bureaucrat. Arrogant executives were competent but generally disliked. Jokes about them were only told in their absence. Benign bureaucrats were deemed incompetent and were shown little respect. They were the butt of a lot of jokes, even in their presence, and were perceived as powerless to do anything about the jokes despite their formal authority.

Jokes about group members coming from either of these types were considered offensive, though for different reasons. With benign bureaucrats, it was because they were not respected as productive members of the group. With arrogant executives, on the other hand, it was simply because they were not liked. They were considered, because of their haughtiness, to have forfeited the 'right' to joke with and about others.

A third important category were the so-called solid citizens. These were the informal group leaders, though they had no official authority. They enjoyed special privileges and dispensations and were allowed to joke about group members, even in their presence, without causing offence. In fact, being joked about by this central figure was welcomed as a sign of acceptance. But solid citizens also had to demonstrate the good grace and robustness to take a joke.

WHO DESERVES HEALTHY DISRESPECT

*"I don't want more money.
I don't want more power.
I want more respect."*

Duncan explained, 'These findings suggest that group status is less a determinant of one's position in the joking pattern than is one's role in the larger social network' (Duncan and Feisal, 1989, p.28).

Novices generally find themselves sidelined from all this activity. Since they are powerless they tend not to be joked about, but nor are they allowed to make jokes at the expense of established group members. This exclusion period can be important for socialization purposes. The novice has a chance to determine who wields the power and how. But not until others start to mock the novice will he or she feel like a real member of the group.

If novices are those with least impact on humorous proceedings, those who have the most are the corporate leaders.

THE HUMOUR OF POWER

Leaders can have a hefty influence on the nature and incidence of corporate humour. They are the custodians of corporate well-being and, depending on their approach, may be the font or the object of much humour.

The arrogant and self-important will feel personally threatened by humour because it will be used behind their backs to puncture their egotism. That is why they may be prompted to denounce it as frivolous and light-minded. The more self-assured will use it as a tool to dispel nervousness in subordinates and to make themselves more approachable; to create a climate of involvement and to enhance team spirit. According to Sir Brian Wolfson:

> Leadership acts as a catalyst to humour. If the leader either has no sense of humour or else is not prepared to get involved, there will be no humour. If the leader has a sense of humour there will be humour, maybe gentle, but people will respond to it. And if he or she is prepared to take an initiative, there will be a lot of humour.

THOSE WHO SET THE TONE

"We're one big happy family here, Jessop, and I have it on good authority you're a miserable bastard."

Leaders can therefore be seen as having a liberating effect on their entourage, who may be carried along in their humorous slip-stream. Indeed, their impact on the company may be such that they leave a humorous legacy behind them. Sir Allen Sheppard acknowledges the influence of his predecessor on the prevailing ethos at GrandMet:

Maxwell Joseph was funny in, say, an AGM, because you could guarantee that he could say something that was tangential to what one expected, not the formal sort of response. He had a very open style simply because he had such a low boredom threshold. If he started reciting a formal statement, he'd get bored after 20 seconds, so he'd start to ad lib, and that sort of ad lib has become a hallmark of the company since his departure.

Thus the humorous contribution of leaders may be accentuated by the fact that they tend to attract like-minded people to the company. As Maxwell Joseph drew Sheppard, so has Sheppard drawn others – executives such as the finance director with whom Sheppard has vowed to 'form a variety act if the company finally goes bust'. Winston Fletcher confesses a similar weakness:

I would always look for humour in a business partner. I think it would be too much to hope that everyone you recruited would be an S. J. Perelman – a bit much in a partner too – but it is certainly the case that nearly all my senior colleagues over the years have been witty. The one exception, who tried to be but wasn't, was quite a strain.

Sir Brian Wolfson echoes that view:

The chemistry of the way people work together is such that you tend to draw to you people with whom you have a level of comfort. If humour is important to you, you cannot work with humourless people around you.

An important consideration, then, in building a management team may be a sense of humour. Those who value it should perhaps screen candidates for signs of a humour bypass. In selection interviews, some feel for likely fit with the rest of the team could be gleaned by throwing in a question about favourite comedy films or comedians. An unexpected answer need not lead to elimination, but might warrant further investigation. The aim is not to appoint a machine-gunning jokester but to avoid a passion killer. As Sir Brian Wolfson saw it:

People without humour are energy sappers, whilst people with humour are energy generators. It can be very draining to find yourself talking to somebody who's po-faced. You get uncomfortable, you want to throw something. Anything just to get a reaction out of them.

The aim in all this is for leaders to create not a one-liner culture but rather one of involvement and trust. By laughing at imperfections in themselves, leaders open up the way to a more honest dialogue. Their readiness to admit their own limitations makes them seem more human and approachable. It conveys the leader's willingness to learn, fumble and persevere.

Take, for instance, the head of an under-resourced maintenance department faced with the annual works shutdown, when the two-week plant overhaul is due to take place. He tells the workers that he feels 'like a mosquito in a nudist camp. I know what's expected, but I haven't a clue where to start'. His humorous admission shows an appreciation of the task ahead. He is effectively saying, 'It's a big challenge but we're all in this together.' He is not claiming to be an all-knowing oracle but rather is declaring his receptiveness to suggestions.

This demonstrates the bonding properties of humour, its ability to establish emotional proximity between leader and followers. It helps to break down barriers between people and promotes a climate which is conducive to open debate. Humour allows people to speak up, to broach delicate subjects and to attack sacred cows. It promotes a healthy exchange of ideas. People will make more daring suggestions, safe in the knowledge that they will not be penalized for it. Humour makes an organization more participative and responsive. With the possibility of humour comes the possibility of challenge and openness to change. Sir Brian Wolfson commented, 'Any company which has humour has far more likelihood of having a culture which is disrespectful, and therefore able to attack change, endure change, and flourish in change.'

Furthermore, when they joke with others, leaders demonstrate that they look upon those people as something more than just a resource to get things done. Leaders who see motivation in terms of sticks and carrots implicitly think of those they are trying to mobilize as donkeys. When people are viewed like that, they are inclined to behave accordingly. To arouse deeper commitment, leaders have to show something of themselves. They have to provide the stimulus that turns a group of individuals into a team. Humour, as Sir John Harvey-Jones sees it, can be the key:

Laughter is a great aid to team building, and if you intend to run your business in a moderately light-hearted manner it is extremely difficult for one of those, fortunately few, beings who have no sense of humour at all to, so to speak, 'join the club'.

(Harvey-Jones, 1988, p.198)

WINDING UP COMPANIES

Corporate humour is not always confined to the boundaries of the organization. It can sometimes be used externally in the fight to gain an edge over competitors. A nice example is the black humour displayed by the executives of Universal Studios in the battle with Walt Disney Studios. This is how the *Financial Times* reported it:

> The intense rivalry between the new $630m Universal Studios theme park in Orlando, Florida, and its well-entrenched Walt Disney rival has taken a macabre and bloody turn. The Universal Studio park includes a spectacular attraction based on the film *Jaws*. As tourists ride by, a 24ft mechanised shark snaps up a pleasure boat. Among the body bits, tee shirts and other flotsam that rise to the surface of the artificial lagoon is a pair of Mickey Mouse ears.
>
> (*Financial Times*, 10 May 1990, p.24)

Or again, at a time when Fuji and Konica were spending heavily abroad, Kodak decided to attack them on their domestic market front through a series of well-worked stunts:

> Kodak's cheekiest ploy was to spend $1 million on an airship emblazoned with its logo. It cruised over Japanese cities for three years, mischievously circling over Fuji's Tokyo headquarters from time to time. To Fuji's chagrin, Japanese newspapers gleefully picked up the story. The Japanese firm was forced to spend twice as much bringing its own airship back from Europe for just two months of face-saving promotion in Tokyo.
>
> Half of all Japanese consumers can now recognise Kodak's goods instantly. Kodak's recent growth puts it within sight of second-place Konica in Japan's market for camera film.
>
> (*The Economist*, 10 November, 1990)

There is something amusingly surreal about corporate giants devoting vast sums to playful one-upmanship. Yet it is not just the sums involved that provide the comic edge. The mere idea of corporations cheekily needling each other and behaving like people is funny. On a smaller scale, for instance, the *Daily Telegraph* engaged in a similar show of brazenness, having just swiped the *Alex* cartoon strip from the *Independent*. This is how Andrew Moncur described it in the *Guardian*:

> The *Daily Telegraph*, not content to poach a cartoon strip from a competitor, has been running an ad campaign knocking its aggrieved rival. These have been described as the sort of ads you'd like to take out at dawn and put up against a wall. And what happens next, just about capping it all? A truck fitted out as a mobile hoarding appears and parks outside the *Independent*'s front door. This trumpets the Daily Dreadnought's triumph in the cartoon war. Eventually it is towed away.
>
> (*Guardian*, 22 January 1992, p.19)

Such antics are of value in promoting competition with rival firms. Putting one over on an adversary is a signal to customers and employees alike. By its jokey character it virtually guarantees media coverage and, even if it doesn't make the national newspapers, it is bound to become part of the industry folklore.

BEYOND CORPORATE CULTURE

Beyond the solidarity born of shared corporate humour there are further, if weaker allegiances. At one remove, there is the culture of particular industrial sectors. Like groups of individuals, agglomerations of companies are apt to nominate their own scapegoats. Each industrial sector has its so-called 'Mickey Mouse' companies. Take the example of the publishing industry. As Giles Gordon put it:

> The cheapest and surest way of raising a laugh in any book trade gathering is to mention André Deutsch, especially in the context of meanness. Everybody gaffaws, not because the diminutive Hungarian is meaner than certain other publishers but because he is a much loved institution.
>
> (*Punch*, 20 May 1988, p.52)

Every industry has its own André Deutsch. Just as groups of individuals need their scapegoats, so industrial sectors need standard butts for their humour. These are the cues by which to identify a fellow insider, someone who knows the score and can't be messed around. Different sectors end up with different norms and values. Advertising is culturally remote from banking; textiles from cars; retailing from pharmaceuticals. These dominant values in an industry affect norms about secrecy, political stance, dress, acceptable behaviour – and they are continuously transmitted in the everyday banter. Novelist David Lodge observes, 'I think all industries have their absurdities which are not visible to the people who work in those industries. They take it all for granted. It's part of the professional mystique or professional jargon.'

Another feature that groups of companies share with groups of individuals is that cohesiveness is often enhanced by focusing on common threats. A whole industry can be mobilized by pointing out the menace posed by foreign competition, government legislation, and so on. Frequently, the threat can be best exposed by means of humour focusing on bureaucratic waste in government regulation, the quality of imports or other such targets.

Consider, for instance, the proposed introduction of legislation requiring American fast-food operators to inform customers of the nutritional contents of each product (*Reynolds*, 1989, p.59). Fearing that this would increase costs and scare off health-conscious customers, the National Restaurants Association decided that the best way to fight the labelling legislation was to poke fun at it. They went straight for the proposal's weakest point, namely the proliferation of labels it would entail. The campaign generated a number of tongue-in-cheek stories and columns by pizza lovers in the press and, as a result of the public ridicule, the labelling legislation was quietly shelved – the victim of a sneer campaign.

The identity of a sector is further strengthened by disparaging other sectors with whom there is rivalry or on which there is dependence. Take, for instance, the relationship between small business owners and banks. *Punch* took a shot at the banking community on behalf of small businesses:

Ineptitude on the scale practised by our banks is not something that you can produce at the drop of a hat. It has to be built up over generations, has to be passed by word of mouth from one banker to another. Such crassness and incompetence should not be allowed to die out. Who is going to notice if another few thousand small businesses go to the wall?

(*Punch*, 11 June 1991, p.20)

That institutionalized hatred can be seen at ground level with the example of a small businessman who went to his bank manager for a loan. Having discovered the conditions under which the bank was prepared to lend him the money, he thanked the bank manager, smiled thinly and told him, 'It gives a whole new meaning to the phrase "bank robbery", don't you think?'

Or again, consider the schism between the City and industry. To burlesque the situation, industrial managers are characterized as boring beer drinkers with cowpat haircuts and cheap suits, while their counterparts in the City are Pims-sipping, Porsche-driving stock-swindlers. The clearest expression of this cultural, social and monetary divide came when the City experienced its redundancy drama in December 1989. Outside the Square Mile, the announcement of hefty lay-offs by Morgan Grenfell and other banks was greeted with amusement and smugness.

Of course, these differences will be put aside when wider 'tribes' are invoked. British managers of whatever calling are also part of the British corporate culture – comrades in arms, striving to increase the wealth of the nation while fighting off foreign incursors. At this level too there is a self image which is reinforced by collective humour – and the mocking of others.

One of the prime targets for jokes is Japan. The businesslike behaviour of the Japanese is constantly derided by outsiders, perhaps as a means of coping with their success. There is the apocryphal story, for instance, of a British businessman abroad who met a Japanese counterpart at the swimming pool of the hotel where both happened to be staying. They got talking and discovered that they were in the same line of business, at which point the Japanese manager reached into his trunks and whipped out ... a waterproof business card.

This idea of Japanese single-mindedness is also expressed by the writer Georges Mikes who cuttingly suggests, 'If they are told that a sense of humour is a desirable proclivity, they will form serious study groups to discover how to acquire a really robust sense of humour' (Mikes, 1970, p.16).

And where do jokes about the Japanese find their natural home? Not in Britain which, though it may deride Japanese efficiency, regards alliances with Japan as a means of redressing its trade balance in manufacturing goods. It is in America that the Japanese threat is most biting. The US has seen its manufacturing supremacy eroded in virtually every sector, including that symbol of Americana, the automobile industry. So widespread is the popular resentment that a cartoon in the *Harvard Business Review* (Nov–Dec 1988, p.127) pretended to institutionalize it: the cartoon showed the exterior of a bar displaying a window sign, 'Japan-bashing hour: 5–7 p.m'.

Sometimes the tribes transcend national boundaries. The expatriate community, for instance, is known to have a fairly pronounced fun culture. Technicians, demolition experts, aid workers and engineers of various nationalities all come together under the banner of humour. National origins are cast aside, with expatriates focusing instead on their homogeneity: the fact that they are drawn from high-income, high-status occupations, that they have common schooling and that they are cosmopolitan in outlook. The whole experience is hyped with a 'we're all in the same boat' and 'let's have fun abroad' disposition, and easy camaraderie blooms. These communities offer the chance to get together with other non-nationals to denounce the place they find themselves in, tell psycho-release stories about the dreadful blunders made in the first week of the posting, and endlessly anecdotalize the 'quaint little ways' of the locals.

Of course, once national cultures have been subsumed, what is left? What bigger tribe can we possibly join? Ultimately it boils down to just two tribes, men and women.

MEMBERS ONLY

Women in organizations often view humour with some suspicion, for it helps to preserve male ascendancy and provides an easy cover for discrimination.

Men in organizations tend to prefer the company of other men. The use of humour between men serves to maintain solidarity on the shop-floor, just as it cultivates clubbishness in the boardroom. A striking manifestation of this convoluted bonding process is the 'ever-ready, and "respectable", almost polite, willingness to notice sexual innuendo in organizational situations, jokes, words' (Hearn and Parkin, 1987, p.158).

Women may disrupt relations within an all-male group. They complicate interaction. For one thing, they inhibit sexist banter or horseplay. For another, the everyday physical contact between male managers cannot be spontaneously expressed when one of the managers is a female. Touch becomes a social hurdle.

Women are therefore seen as representing a threat to male

bonding. It follows that men, consciously or not, use humour to keep women out or to put them down.

Few women have not had a supposedly funny sexist remark made at their expense. Barbs which are clearly meant to cause discomfort or to undermine credibility can be dealt with head on or reported. More difficult to handle is the everyday banter which has a dubious edge. The crime is often indefinable and the intention uncertain. For instance, when one managing director telephoned a colleague to enquire as to the progress of a newly appointed female executive, he was told, 'As it happens, she's sitting on my lap. Would you like to speak to her?' The woman, who was standing in his office at the time, immediately found herself cast in a subservient role, not really to be taken seriously except as an executive perk.

Similarly, Jeff Hearn referred to a conversation between male lecturers in the office of one of their secretaries:

Lecturer A: Have you got an ashtray here?

Lecturer B: (on home territory) Oh yes, there's one here. Susie smokes non-stop.

Lecturer A: But it's empty.

Lecturer B: She's off today. Geraldine doesn't smoke. She hasn't any vices, have you Geraldine? (laughter all round)

(Hearn and Parkin, 1987, p.125)

The point Hearn makes is that this conversation took place in Geraldine's office during an 'invasion' by five men. It is difficult to imagine Geraldine speaking to lecturer B in this way without her behaviour being construed as 'brazen'. The direction of sexual innuendo therefore serves to reinforce power relations. It is a routine way of maintaining authority and is thoroughly embedded in the culture of the organization. The aside may appear innocuous, innocent even, but this merely contributes to its insidious power – any woman who 'kicks up a fuss' about it will merely attract ridicule. Her protests will be jokingly dismissed as evidence of awkwardness, crankiness, even paranoia.

Or take the reverse experience of a female boss, Jean Denton. On her first day as Director of External Affairs for the Austin Rover Group, a male subordinate greeted her by saying, 'I've worked for two women before – one was my mother and one was my wife' (Bryce, 1989, p.65).

What is an appropriate response? To admonish the perpetrator would leave her open to the indictment that she was hypersensitive or 'couldn't take a joke' – is there a worse fate in Britain than being branded humourless? Indeed, that very fear might even compel a woman to feign a smile and treat the comment as though it really were meant playfully – as does the social pressure to put on a smile when a joke eludes us.

Ignoring the comment, then, might be the most expeditious option, but it is likely to prove frustrating as well as suggesting an inability to take control.

An alternative would be to play dumb and ask, 'What do you mean by that?' thereby giving the perpetrator a chance to back down. But this too could backfire, perhaps making it look as though she could not understand a joke, never mind take one.

Given these unattractive options, it may be best to fight fire with fire in order to re-establish who is in charge. At worst, there is the possibility of sarcasm. A cheerful 'I'm honoured' or 'Thank you', as though the remark were meant as a genuine compliment, would at least thwart the attempt to embarrass.

But the ideal response would be a cutting riposte which has all the playful ambiguity of the opening gambit. Something like: 'I'm surprised there've been *two* women in your life.'

The problem for women as regards exploiting humour in this way is that they have been socialized to react to humour rather than initiate it. For a woman to tell a joke, she must violate the cultural expectation that females should not aggressively dominate mixed-sex social interaction. This idea was confirmed by Eve Pollard, editor of the *Sunday Express*, herself no wallflower:

> I think that women are in fact very funny, but they've kept it a great secret from men because men don't like women laughing at other women's jokes, they like us to laugh at men's jokes. It's not our role to be funny.

There is a tendency in organizations to value men's humour over women's humour. The same behaviour from men and women tends, therefore, to be interpreted quite differently: he's funny, she's frivolous; he's a raconteur, she's a gossip; he's sharp, she's catty; he's zany, she's unhinged; and he might be serious, but she's uptight.

The kinds of traits which would earn a young man a reputation for having the right stuff for promotion are apt to damage a young woman's career, or at least serve as justification for passing her over for promotion. Consider the testimony of Anthea Ballam who quit her job in a hierarchic organization in order to set up her own PR agency:

> I think I may have been held down because I was facetious. I mean nobody's going to say, 'We're not promoting you because you're a woman.' They say other things. And the fact that I might have made flippant comments in the past, is a good reason for them not to trust you, and to question your commitment.

Thus many strong, self-willed women are weeded out at an early stage. The fear that being light-hearted may brand them as being lightweight persuades others to suppress their sense of humour. Those who are ambitious sometimes find that they have to bite their tongues rather than frighten men by demonstrating their wit. As Janet Daley explains:

> Women who 'get on' in hierarchical institutions are the sort of women whom men like to work with. And what men want from women at work is flattery (not necessarily in the crude sense — just an acknowledgement of their unquestioned authority) and the kind of competent perceptiveness that oils the wheels of office life. More than anything, perhaps, they want women who are prepared whenever necessary to cease to exist.
>
> (*The Times*, 10 March 1992, p.14)

Women in organizations, then, find themselves in a Catch-22 situation: if they instigate humour, they are usurping a male role; and if they do not, they are deemed to be lacking something. Theirs is simply to appreciate. But even this has its drawbacks for women. As *Sunday Express* editor, Eve Pollard, points out, 'The signals which make for a good working relationship between men can spell danger for women. If a woman smiles too readily, she can be misinterpreted.'

Self-effacing invisibility may seem like the safest option, but ultimately it also prevents women from assuming key positions. The alternative is to dare to be different. Humour is risky, but it is also a vital means of influence and an assertion of authority. Harnessing the power of humour can help women to get their way.

TALKING OUT OF TURN

"That's an excellent suggestion, Miss Triggs.
Perhaps one of the men here would like to make it."

Lee Bryce (1989, p.94) relates the experience of a senior executive applying for a job on which she had missed the cut-off date. The company had already finished interviewing and had drawn up a short-list, but they agreed to see her since she was 'just round the corner'.

During the interview they told her, 'We'll have to confess that, good though you are, we were really looking for a chap. This is a very male-orientated organization. The other staff are all men.'

'Well,' came back the answer, 'I can wear a suit and tie, and speak in a low voice, but I can't grow a beard.'

With humour, she made her point as well as exhibiting poise under pressure. She also conveyed self-confidence and resourcefulness. Their fears that she might have problems dealing with men were shown to be unfounded and she later got the job.

Another job candidate's timely injection of humour was cited by humour consultant, Malcolm Kushner:

During the interview the male interviewer – a 'macho good old boy' – asked if she had any children. The female interviewer instantly became pale and nervous. And with good reason. Asking that question during a job interview is a violation of federal laws against employment discrimination. My friend solved the problem with her sense of humour. She replied, 'None that I know of.'

(Kushner, 1990, p.24)

Her answer indicated to one interviewer that she would not be issuing them with a lawsuit and to the other that she was no cipher. She too got the job.

Barbara Young, chief executive of the Royal Society for the Protection of Birds and previously district general manager of one of the largest health authorities in Britain, also used humour to make an impact:

When I saw the RSPB advertisement I wrote saying, 'I bet you can't afford me. I know the front end of a bird from the back, and that's all — but I'm a competent manager.' After a succession of interviews where they said I wasn't quite what they were looking for, they offered me the job.

(*Sunday Times Magazine,* 22 March 1992, p.86)

This idea of overcoming prejudice with humour was taken further by a female executive *d'un certain age.* She explained, 'You reach a stage in your life where you are fighting both sexism and ageism – and of the two, ageism is the bigger barrier. There's a lot of truth in the old chestnut that employers won't look at a woman over 40, unless it's the bust size.'

Given that dual handicap she has had to work harder to get interviews, and experience has shown that humour can help: 'I've found that instead of disguising the fact that I was well over 40, it was better to come straight out with it. So when I write off for jobs, I will use the analogy of a vintage car: built for reliability, rather than sleekness and speed, portraying myself as someone who is going to stay the course. And that approach has opened quite a few doors.'

The ploy elicits curiosity from employers, and transforms age into a selling point. But rather than earnestly saying, 'I am terribly dependable' she puts it across in a tongue-in-cheek way. Yet the ability of humour to transcend the gender gap has its limits, as she sees it: 'It's like the post-3M joke, which stands for post-*matrimony,* post-*motherhood* and post-*menopause*. On that basis you don't have to take time off for the kids, you're not caught up with romance, and you're past sex and headaches. It would be a viable way of reinforcing your suitability for a job. But that's more of a joke to use among women, rather than with men.'

Eve Pollard endorses the view that certain forms of humour do not go down well with men:

It's very rare for women to make such crude jokes as men, but when I have made jokes with a sexual connotation, I've found that men get uneasy. It poses too great a threat to a man's sense of masculinity and presumed confidence. So there's no humorous version of equal opportunities.

Thus, while society places restrictions on women in their use of humour, it remains a vital tool. It can help push women to the fore, and help them parry the 'playful' chauvinism they encounter on their way up. Humour is also a forceful channel for exposing the ingrained sexism in many organizations.

THE MUFFIA

"I'm sorry, Mr Aldgate, I'm afraid the bulge in your crotch isn't big enough."

The fact remains that jokes such as the one on page 123 are only funny because they subvert the stereotype. Our very laughter is a poignant reminder of the hurdles, humorous or otherwise, impeding the managerial progress of women. Without incongruity there would be no humour.

Advertising's Talent to Amuse

6

It is more palatable, certainly in Britain, to put across sales messages if you do it with a smile. You can convince people of quite hard sell propositions if you put them to people in a charming, light-hearted, likeable way.

(Winston Fletcher, chairman, Bozell Europe)

Earlier, in Chapter 2, the point was made that organizations are allegedly sexless places. Everyone knows that sex influences organizational behaviour, but no one dares admit it. Yet the role of sex *is* acknowledged near the organizational boundaries. For instance, many companies consider sex a legitimate aspect of advertising, promotion and 'public relations'. Receptions and trade fairs, brochures and business calendars may make use of sex in promoting the company and its products. Above all, sex often lands the lead role in commercials, whether for cosmetics or for computers.

The same is true of humour. It too is marginalized, only being officially sanctioned near the organization's boundaries. It is at the interface with consumers that humour comes into its own. Sales patter often includes scripted witticisms and presentations, at least in Anglo-Saxon countries, invariably kick off with a joke. However, as with sex, humour finds its greatest expression in advertising.

The way that humour is used within companies to influence and unite individuals is echoed externally. Many companies use humour in their advertising as a device for targeting, segmenting and persuading consumers. Advertising is one of the few domains where humour is not just authorized but encouraged. And increasingly so.

AD NAUSEAM

Until the late 1970s, British TV commercials were mostly character-ized by their brashness. There were isolated funny campaigns – notably Guinness and PG Tips – but these were the exception rather than the rule. The idea was for the advertiser to fire as many mentions of the product as possible in the space of half a minute. The viewer's senses were beset by garish images, bold lettering, inane jingles, patronizing voice-overs and crass product claims. The theory was mostly elementary Freud, and even when the advertise-ments were not crammed with psycho-sexual symbols, viewers saw them. Wary of manipulation, they became resistant to the propositions.

ON THE OFFENSIVE

ZAPP!!
NOW WITH
ADDED
EXCLAMATION
MARKS!

The traditionally percussive relationship between advertiser and viewer has since mellowed. Advertising has seen the demise of the conventional frontal assault in favour of a sort of Trojan-horse approach, where the well-packaged commercial subtly sheds its brand load to ferment in the consumer's unsuspecting mind. Typically, the new-look commercials are short on information content or even persuasion of the orthodox 'lasts twice as long' genre, but they are heavy on style and humour.

Many commercials today barely mention the product. Instead, the allotted thirty seconds are used to set up an elaborate sketch, either comical or dramatic. Selling is no longer a question of brainwashing viewers but rather of grabbing their attention. The idea is for consumers to take the commercial (the surrogate product) to heart. Attachment to brands is considered to be as much emotional as rational. Consumers buy a particular brand because of the way it makes them feel. A commercial therefore has to have soul.

The drift away from the tried and tested 'slam it home' style of advertising has occurred for a variety of reasons – not least because consumers were getting fed up with hard sell. Loud, crude, cheap commercials which pounded the brand name and product use – such as the American example 'With Hirschfields haemorrhoid treatment you'll sit more comfortably' – probably work if viewers are prepared to pay attention, but not if they have already switched off (figuratively or literally). By the mid-1970s this intrusive and irritating approach elicited justifiable disdain from most viewers.

There was another precipitating factor behind the change. Imagine our reaction today if the entire commercial break were filled with advertisements of the 'We soaked one half in new improved *Shifto* and the other half in bitumen . . .' type. We would quite simply swap channels. But in the 1970s, when controls were manual, it was a case of asking Mum to flick it over on her way out to put the kettle on.

The subsequent invasion of the nation's households by the video recorder and its sidekick, the remote control device, has had quite an impact on audience viewing behaviour. A verbal manifestation of that impact was the emergence of two evocative terms, zipping and zapping. Zipping occurs when the viewer uses the fast-forward facility on a pre-recorded programme in order to skip past the commercials. Zapping has the same end but refers to the channel-switching which often accompanies commercial breaks during live viewing. Commercial dodging was made easy since avoidance no longer demanded a physical effort from the viewer. It became possible to wipe out millions of pounds' worth of advertising at the flick of a switch.

Suddenly the television audience could be more discriminating in its choice of viewing. Advertisers could no longer trade on the laziness of the average viewer. Instead they had actively to engage the interest of viewers and persuade them to stay tuned. For the newly empowered viewer it became a case of amuse me or lose me.

PASSIVE VIEWING

"Damn! The remote control's out of reach."

FROM JUNK ADS TO AD JUNKIES

For the companies which pay for the advertising, the swing towards entertaining campaigns is of some concern. While accepting that quirkiness helps their thirty-second short to stand out from the crowd, they are understandably worried that commercial advocacy has taken a back seat.

It is true that the abrasive, hard sell of the 1960s and early 1970s was probably better suited to emblazoning a message on the viewer's mind. But this is a moot point since a generalized return to that approach would merely undermine the popular following which commercials now command. Where people used to deride commercials they will now sit through them, comment on them, even look out for them. Britain has become a nation of advertising buffs.

Previously, advertising was considered a parasitical spin-off of 'real' television entertainment. Today, the vignettes that make up the Heineken campaign, for instance, are a British comic institution which is arguably as established as any long-running sitcom. The Wordsworth advertisement in particular stands out as one of the best examples of how to use thirty seconds of film. The scene opens with Wordsworth in a Cumbrian landscape, moodily groping for the first line of 'Daffodils' ('Er ... er ... I was just strolling around, not doing very much ... er ... er') and only finding it ('I wandered, lonely as a cloud') after taking an inspiring draught of Heineken. This was followed by the clinching, pun-pretty line: 'Heineken refreshes the poets other beers cannot reach'.

What has been lost by impoverished brand name-dropping has been gained by an increased and more attentive audience. Again this is a point of some controversy. On the one hand, there is research evidence to suggest that entertaining commercials do a 'generic job' for the product. This means that competitors gain spill-over benefits from one company's advertising. A good example was the widely acclaimed Creature Comforts campaign featuring engaging Plasticine animals. Many viewers associated the campaign with British Gas rather than the intended beneficiary, the electricity companies.

On the other hand, it is claimed that the traditional market research methods cannot really cope with the new-style commercials. The argument is that common measuring techniques, relying on instant recall, do not do justice to the more esoteric advertisements which are often absorbed in a more impressionistic way. The implication is that the quality of the measuring instruments must keep pace with the increased sophistication of the message, as well as the increasing discrimination of the viewing public.

Today, the average British viewer watches nearly three hours of commercials every week, the equivalent of two feature films. Such exposure has guaranteed that consumers are no longer the impressionable recipients of propaganda described in Vince Packard's book *The Hidden Persuaders* (1960).

Consumers have grown much more sophisticated in their understanding of advertising – so much so that many commercials, clapperboards to the fore, actually invite viewers to laugh at the advertising process itself. Advertising literacy is high in Britain. Consumers happily describe products as 'up-' or 'down-market' rather than in traditional class or quality terms; they use words like 'promote', 'demonstrate', 'image' and 'awareness'. Advertising agencies have found that their test audiences can not only decode exactly what the commercial is trying to say, but also how it is trying to say it. Winston Fletcher is sensitive to the change:

> I have sat in a market research group among East Anglian farm labourers when they looked at roughs of commercials and said, 'That would make a good lager ad, but it wouldn't do for bitter. You've got the wrong strategy there. If you're really selling bitter you've got to have some more traditional values, because bitter isn't lighthearted like lager. It's a more serious thing altogether.' You get a lot of sophisticated playback from the public. Whether this happens in other countries, I don't know. But certainly in Britain, people think about, talk about and analyse advertising.

The viewing public is not only aware of the games that advertisers play, but it actually enjoys these games. Every viewer is an armchair critic, judging the style, content and effectiveness of the advertisements, irrespective of the relevance of the product to the individual.

In many ways, then, the communication process between advertiser and viewer has undergone a complete turn-round. Previously, advertising was obsessed with *emission*, leaving the brand's indelible imprint on the viewer's mind while showing scant regard for entertainment value. Today, commercials focus on the process of *reception*. They try to seduce us in oblique ways. They do not, as a matter of course, enumerate claims up front, but sidle up to us and entice us into mental collaboration. And humour is a particularly effective way of achieving this.

SELLING WITH A SMILE

Humour is suited to communicating an advertising message for three reasons. First, commercials have economy forced on them: air time costs money. Humour also places a premium on brevity. Like advertising, humour requires stylized emphasis. The humorist exaggerates the relevant aspects of reality, but simplifies or omits those elements which might side-track the attention of the audience.

The discipline of compression also characterizes the approach of the advertising copy-writer who minimizes anything which might distract consumers from the product. Former JWT chairman Jeremy Bullmore cites the example of the advertisement produced in America when Volkswagen introduced the Rabbit (known as the Golf in the UK):

> There were two live rabbits looking straight at the camera, with their noses and whiskers, as rabbits do. And then it said, 'In 1956 there were only two VWs in America.' It lasted 10 seconds, and made its case with economy and wit.
>
> *(Sunday Times,* 13 September 1992, p.8.5)

THE GREATEST COPYWRITER

Second, humour serves the ends of advertising through its capacity to reveal. Humour makes people think, it opens their minds and makes them see the familiar from an unfamiliar viewpoint. Since the recurrent challenge of advertising is to show everyday products in a new light, humour is easily annexed to that cause. As Jeremy Bullmore put it, 'At its best humour is revelatory. So the conscientious use of humour in advertising allows people to see the merits of a product or a brand without it being drilled into them.'

A good joke, like a good advertisement (judged purely in terms of its communications effectiveness), should allow those on the receiving end to see something for themselves – which introduces the idea of audience participation.

The third reason for using humour in advertising is that it

involves. Humour is not just about making every word count; it is also about implicitness. Unless the viewer makes the necessary act of completion, there is no joke:

Question: What is the difference between a dead hedgehog and a dead taxman in the middle of the road?
Answer: There are skid marks in front of a hedgehog.

The reader has to make an intellectual contribution in order to 'see the joke'. If the answer to the joke had been 'The driver didn't slow down for the taxman' the sentiment is the same, but the joke is lost. The idea that taxmen are despicable is implied, but an imaginative effort is needed to make that connection. When the reader is spared the effort, the comic effect evaporates. Denied the chance to participate, there is no flash-moment of perception and pleasure.

Involvement, then, requires hints in lieu of statements. A humorous narrative leaves gaps to be filled by the receiver. Arthur Koestler believed that the wider these gaps, 'the more will the consumer's reactions approximate the producer's – whose mental effort he is compelled to re-create' (Koestler, 1964, p.94).

The copy-writer's skill lies in making sure that the creative gap left for the viewer to bridge is neither too narrow nor too wide. Jeremy Bullmore cites an example:

The Hamlet campaign is a subtle combination of words, music and pictures. The words are almost superfluous because you know what's happened by the time you hear that music and it's confirmed when you're told, 'Happiness is a cigar called Hamlet.' You do all the work: you realize what's going on; you see frustration; you see the pack, you see the light, you see the smoke, and the music tells you that it's better. The best example is the ad with the golfer who can't get out of the bunker. All you hear is a match being struck and a puff of smoke – incidentally, they claimed they had Laurence Olivier in that bunker. That is the perfect Hamlet commercial because you don't see anything, you contribute it all.

These close parallels between the principles of humour and those of commercial persuasion prompted Bullmore to write, 'In the pursuit of better advertisements, there is probably more to be learned from a study of the anatomy of humour than from any other subject' (Bullmore, 1991, p.65).

SUCKERS FOR THE SAME CAMPAIGNS

Contemporary viewers are expected to think for themselves, the rationale being that if they get the joke they will be inclined to buy the product or, at least, remember the brand name.

Many advertisements are designed to appeal to a certain mind set: that is, to groupings which share the same tastes and opinions without necessarily sharing the same social or income band. Such advertising is not for 'general consumption', but rather a *point de repère* for like-minded people. Viewers are invited to join the conspiracy by identifying with the humorous cues in the commercial.

Beer advertising typifies this approach. Target viewers are seduced by commercials which acknowledge their attitudes and sense of humour, and only theirs, without making concessions to anyone else's. Beneath the comic hyperbole of Heineken's miraculous claims or Carling Black Label's super-feats is a disarmingly affectionate send-up of everything that the in-crowd finds attractive about itself.

Take a memorable lager commercial as an example. A mind-reader was performing a cabaret act, and had already proved to be spot-on with two members of the audience. The camera turned to the familiar faces of the two regular protagonists. One turned to the other and started, 'Here . . .' The mind-reader quickly broke in, 'Yes, I do', thereby pre-empting the usual comment, 'I bet he drinks Carling Black Label.' Here again we see the need for completion, without which there is no joke. But increasingly, the only people capable of completing the joke are those familiar with 'the campaign so far . . .'. Humour is used as a segmenter. The joke makes no sense to outsiders; it will only leave them perplexed.

There is a superiority factor involved too. People want to be flattered, to feel they are in touch. One-upmanship and conspicuous materialism came back into fashion in the 1980s, and the advertisers went out of their way to appeal to isolated segments of society, as epitomized by the self-consciously obscure Guinness ('It's not easy being a dolphin') advert. It was an approach emulated by Holsten Pils – complete with enigmatic star (Jeff Goldblum) and nonsensical anagrams ('stops in hell') – and then repeated in the soft drinks market with the bizarre advertisement featuring a twenty-stone bald genie rushing up to a Tango drinker and planting a kiss on his lips. Such advertisements deliberately exclude those who are not 'in the know', and in doing so the humour is deemed to add to their intrinsic value. The commercials have become social discriminators – with a penchant for the young, metropolitan, style-conscious group of A/B viewers – rather than the levellers they once were. Social groups are defined by the advertisements with which they identify, or by which they are ensnared.

Consumers are pleased to be credited with a modicum of intelligence. They become part authors of the joke when they unlock it. There is a sense of self-congratulation which accompanies the humorous revelation. And no campaign exploited the consumer's own smugness better than Perrier's. Through the 1980s, Perrier became a byword for wit, for social and intellectual snobbery. It is unparalleled in the annals of British advertising.

BEAU JEST

Perhaps to a greater extent than Porsches, hair gel or mobile phones, Perrier mineral water was a totem of the 1980s. The epitome of designer chic, it was a product which sold more on style than substance. No mere fizzy drink capable of quenching the average thirst, it was rather a badge bearing full details of one's place in society.

Perrier's success is a tribute to the power of branding. The company pulled off the not inconsiderable feat of persuading consumers to pay more for a glass of carbonated water than for the same measure of some wines, and even petrol. But there is more to it than that. Smirnoff too sells a tasteless, colourless and virtually odourless fluid at a premium price. The difference is that vodka (more's the pity) does not pour free from taps in every home.

Until Perrier came along, the average British consumer was quite content with the stuff that fell into the sink. It was all right for foreigners to buy bottled water because their own tap water was tainted, unwholesome, not to say foreign. Some Britons on their excursions abroad still feel obliged to spend a mandatory time in bed with gippy tummy as a penance for forgetting to boil the water before cleaning their teeth, showering open-mouthed or taking drinks with ice.

In 1974, then, when Perrier relaunched in Britain, the market for mineral water was less than effervescent. Indeed, a survey conducted at that time by the *Financial Times* pointed out that bottled mineral water was drunk exclusively by 'cranks and foreigners'. Perrier clearly had its work cut out. It was going into a non-existent market with what cynics called a non-existent product. The marketing problems seemed insoluble, so to speak.

Over the following four years, Perrier and its advertising agency, Leo Burnett, addressed the problem of increasing distribution beyond a small circle of posh hotels and wooing a larger audience. In the process, Perrier instigated not only a change in our attitude to the most basic physical requirement – water – but also a sea change in social drinking.

Most of the credit for that turn-round must go to a much-reviled institution, the pun. In 1978 Perrier was advised to use posters as its main advertising medium in the United Kingdom by Leo Burnett, and one of the lines the creative department came up with was 'Eau la la'.

As Perrier established a market for mineral water in the United Kingdom, a number of competitors emerged and the company decided it needed a long-term property for the brand, and so the 'Eau' theme was developed into a whole campaign. The idea was to lock into the growing Francophilia of the British middle classes; to reach people who, according to the advertising agency, 'wanted to project a cultured rather than a *nouveau riche* image'. (The sales pitch 'Not for the Nouveaux' might have been apt.) It was hoped, then, that Perrier water might gatecrash the cheese, wine and slides-from-Provence evenings that cause so much suffering in suburban Britain.

Within a few years, Perrier had captured the sophisticated market and was making inroads on the mass market. The drink benefited from the association with France and therefore with *haute couture*, gourmet cooking and fine wine. Yet it deftly avoided the dismal connotations of teetotalism and sissyism in a way that excruciatingly sweet soft drinks could not. This opened up whole new vistas for the bulbous bottle. It became an indispensable fashion item, an accessory without which no Yuppie lunch was complete. Such was its success that even Coca-Cola got scared and launched a mineral water called Kristal – but as far as habitués of Perrier were concerned this was not *the real thing*. It flopped.

'Eau' provided a shorthand way of saying unique, French and fun. Puns such as 'H2Eau', 'Eauasis', 'Bistreau' and 'Picasseau' not only amused people but massaged the ego of actual and aspiring Perrier drinkers. The consumer had to meet the advertiser half-way by applying a little schoolboy French to an obvious if splendidly art-directed visual pun.

Though minimalist and esoteric, the 'eau' theme was gloriously flexible and could easily be adapted to convey specific benefits on a tactical basis, through the use of such lines as 'N'eau Calories'. The wonderful witticisms encapsulated the brand and the connotations of the brand dominated the product. They trumpeted the exclusivity of Perrier.

Consumers were buying an image, a kudos. Perrier bottled values. Through the 1980s the ubiquitous dark-green bottles became virtually synonymous with 'yuppie' chic. They combined a twist of conspicuous consumption with fashionable green concern about personal health. Asking for a Perrier at a business lunch was about one-upmanship. It was a statement. It said: 'I am in control – I care about my health and I can afford to do so.'

As if the trendy appeal of mineral water were not enough, people began to doubt whether British tap-water was really any better than the ghastly stuff they tried to avoid abroad. The proposed privatization of the water industry led to a thorough investigation of British tap-water, and in 1986 the Consumers' Association esti-mated that up to a quarter was substandard, and infested with cell-devouring, brain-mashing insecticides.

The net result was that the rise in Perrier's turnover and profits through the 1980s was unmatched except by the growth of the property and, lo and behold, advertising firms. But even as Perrier's share prices hit their all-time high, one sensed an impending backlash. The Filofax Company was ailing, as was Sophie Mirman's Sock Shop. The style-obsessed 1980s were coming to a close, and what geaus up . . .

Perrier's own S-eau-S (for May days) advertisement eerily prefigured the impending benzene scare. But the exquisite untimeli-ness of this poster campaign merely corroborated the idea that one aspect of humour in business is the razor's edge between success and failure, and the unerring precision with which companies can shoot themselves in the foot.

EAUN GOAL

(For May days.)

AND IF ONE GREEN BOTTLE . . .

February 1990 saw Perrier beset by a health scare about the purity of its product following the discovery of the cancer-causing chemical, benzene. Sadly, nothing sells newspapers like a health scare, but this one had particular appeal for several reasons:

- First, no one was really at risk since the small traces of benzene would require massive consumption of Perrier water to endanger anyone. Since the risks of eauverdeause were small, the headline-writers had a certain margin for flippancy.

- Second, the witticims that had become a hallmark of Perrier's success could easily be turned against it. This would not be the first time a company had been hoisted by its own advertising slogan. In an earlier contamination scare, the Safeway supermarket chain was embarrassed by its slogan of 'Everything you want from a store and a little bit more'. But this time the idea of a versatile pun to play with introduced a whole new dimension. Indeed, the company had already experienced this in a mild form when admen had coined the 's'eau expensive' pun — but at that time the product was flying high, and mockery merely added to its cachet. It dispelled the ludicrous suggestion that consumers were drinking water because they were too poor to afford anything else.

- Third, there was an added twist in the Perrier case. Journalists are not renowned teetotallers and they, perhaps more than most, had been made to feel morally deficient under the reign of Perrier. Peter Eastcott wrote:

In recent years, one of the most painful features of business lunches at so many formerly sybaritic City tables has been the spectacle of a long row of mineral water glasses, where once the Chief Executive's Château Lynch-Bages was scarcely good enough. There has been an air of moral superiority attached to water, which those of us who find the working day unbearable without the recourse to a modest lunchtime tincture have found hard to take.

(*Daily Telegraph,* 15 February 1990)

This was the chance for journalists to get their own back, to unleash the vitriol accumulated through the 1980s. And with the creative incentive of bilingual word play, one had visions of gleeful journalists positively drooling at the prospect of sticking the boot in.

The fevered imagination of the jaded headline writers from the *Daily Express* and the *Sun* both came up with 'Eau no!', while the *Financial Times* went for 'Bitter pill to swalleau', and the *Sunday Telegraph* asked, 'Is the party eauver?' This last headline was probably the most telling: it hinted at the wider societal impact of the corporate tragedy. A whole culture was crumbling.

The benzene scare sent the company into one of the greatest damage limitation exercises ever undertaken. It withdrew its entire world-wide stocks across 145 countries – a total of 160 million bottles – from wholesalers, distributors and retailers.

It then waited two months to relaunch, with a host of personalities bidding consumers, 'Helleau again' and reminding consumers that it was 'The sole eau'. The brand had taken a battering, but the pun was intact and leading the charge to claw back its market share.

LAUGHING STOCK

The decision to opt for humorous advertising is not one to be taken lightly, since it can so easily backfire. It is primarily through their advertising that companies reveal their personalities to consumers; and the image projected outwards will be reflected back. So, besides its influence on sales, the affection, esteem or otherwise with which the corporate badge is held by consumers has an impact on the company's own employees and on its capacity to attract new recruits. These, in turn, shape the corporate culture.

A STYLE TO FIT THE PRODUCT

ARCO DRUG CO.

SCHWADRun.

RITTERHAUS ADVERTISING

"See here, Ritterhaus, I want TV commercials that will give people headaches and upset-stomachs."

In deciding on the relevance of humour, the nature of the product and the target audience have both to be taken into consideration. A rough guide to the likely scope for humour in commercials is proposed by Jeremy Bullmore:

> Expensive products are not necessarily serious, nor cheap ones frivolous. When you consider the suitability of a humorous approach, it's more important to consider the kind of people you are trying to reach and whether or not the product is bought from discretionary income.

Not surprisingly, products such as beer and cigars have been instrumental in establishing the legitimacy of humour in advertising. The harmful side-effects of such products forced manufacturers to think creatively about how to lighten up their image. Frivolity seems a better marketing strategy for the brewing and tobacco companies than telling consumers about their products, since it would be impossible to evoke the pleasures without blatantly ignoring the consequences. These companies have elected to side-step the problem by focusing not on the product itself but on the trendy people who enjoy it. Jeremy Bullmore expands:

> The very act of saying 'I will have a cigar', 'I will buy a bar of chocolate' is fun. These are agreeable expenditures. You have chosen to make them — not like buying household products or motor oil. Indulgence products lend themselves more naturally to a humorous treatment. The idea of promoting washing powders in a jokey way may appeal to the copywriter, but if you are 29 years old, and you've got 3 kids and not much income, then washing clothes is not funny. It's something you've got to do and you want it to be good, but you don't want to be mocked.

This said, some unlikely companies have jumped on the humour bandwagon. At the forefront has been the financial services sector. Here, the offering has little intrinsic appeal. Who wants to think about death, retirement, hypothetical crises, or even portentous financial decisions? Such services are sold, not bought. They rely on persuasion. To this end, just about every bank or building society has at some time signed up a comic celebrity as brand mascot. Such was the demand that Rowan Atkinson was forced to double up (Prudential and later Barclaycard).

The idea that comedians are consumer-friendly has merit. The problem was that the financial sector seemed overrun with them. When it came to taking action, consumers could not remember which comedian's bank or building society they wanted to visit. The comedians' colonization of the financial sector proved self-defeating for the advertisers.

The surest sign of the pervasiveness of the humorous approach is that even cleaning products, those stalwarts of the hard sell, have got in on the act. Persil washing up liquid secured the services of comedian Robbie Coltrane and his eccentric grandmother to boost its sales, while Domestos Multi Surface Cleaner featured two panic-stricken germs. But the most radical departure was a commercial featuring a well-heeled couple in a restaurant, a hackneyed advertising format. On finishing the meal, the man searched anxiously for his wallet. He eventually reached into his bag and we heard the waiter utter the familiar 'That will do nicely, Sir' – at which point we found out that the man was in fact holding a bottle of Morning Fresh detergent with which he was proposing to do the washing up. The late 1980s saw a surge in spoof advertisements of this kind in which our expectations were dragged one way, then confounded.

THE JOKE WEARS THIN

Parody has become a key weapon of the copy-writers. The commercial credited with establishing the genre was a 1986 Carling Black Label reworking of the Levi jeans launderette classic.

Poking fun at rivals is justified on the grounds that television commercials have so little time to get their message across that mimicry and plagiarism are legitimate short cuts. The idea is to lull viewers into a false sense of security by hinting at, or copying, a campaign with which they are familiar, then subverting the stereotype with a piece of incongruous behaviour.

An easy target has been the sugary images favoured by Coca-Cola and Pepsi which were mocked by both Irn Bru and Schweppes. The Schweppes campaign featured John Cleese. Successive advertisements took viewers through the stages of agreeing an advertising contract with a celebrity, culminating in a full-blown Cola-type singing and dancing jamboree. Only the idiosyncratic presence of John Cleese hamming it up as a hip youngster gave the game away. It was a measure of the confidence that advertisers have in the capacity of viewers to distinguish between joke kitsch and the real thing.

Such parodies indicate a confidence and self-assurance which simply did not exist in the advertising industry fifteen years ago. Elaborate pastiches of other advertisements hinge on the assumption that viewers will already be familiar with the commercial being sent up and that they will be vigilant enough to spot the difference. In the 1970s such an assumption would have been misplaced. Commercials were routinely dismissed as an insult to our intelligence. If we paid any attention to them it was to laugh *at* them, not *with* them. All that has evidently changed. The commercials have even become an accepted subject in polite society.

But there is a disadvantage to taking the spoof route, to hijacking other advertisements and nudge-nudge cross-referencing. Facile humour at another company's expense can become a substitute for creative thinking and a strong message. Resorting to it seems tantamount to admitting that new creativity is impossible, that there can only be exhuming and recycling of the old, that advertisements have reached a cul-de-sac. Jeremy Bullmore concedes that it is all somewhat incestuous:

> Advertising agencies are full of quite bright, quite young people, who have little experience of real life. You have this tiny community of agency people and all they think about is advertising and their heroes are all advertising people – which is why you get too many ads reflecting other ads. That's not a client failing, it's an agency fault.

A LORE UNTO THEMSELVES

"Gosh, thank you, sir! I didn't know advertising **had** annals."

DISAPPEARING UP THEIR OWN ARTISTRY

One of the key reasons that so many agencies are keen to incorporate humour is that it is almost a *sine qua non* for winning the assorted goblets, plaques and trophies that are proudly displayed in agency foyers.

Today there are about twice as many award schemes as there were a decade ago, and three times as many as two decades ago. The number of categories in each award scheme has also mushroomed. The advertising community even has its very own Cannes Film Festival which, in its own industry, is accorded the same prestige as the main festival. As Winston Fletcher says, 'Not even Hollywood at its vainglorious zany zenith could have bettered this bundle of laughable laurels and pompous *palmes d'or* (Fletcher, 1984, p.12).

Advertising festivals tend to include a token sprinkling of 'serious' entrants, often in the public service category – advertising's equivalent of Hollywood's best foreign film – but virtually every category, from best director to best actor, best script to best voice-over, is dominated by funny advertisements. Creative awards invariably go to commercials that the juries find entertaining. Winston Fletcher explains:

> People who produce advertisements like them to be admired by other people who produce advertisements. They're often more interested in the acclaim of their peers and their competitors than they are in whether the advertisements work in the market place. And commercials which are funny tend to be admired by other agency people.

This tug of war between entertainment and commerce, between impressing industry colleagues and flogging goods, is becoming increasingly one-sided. Agencies are straying from their original mission. Jeremy Bullmore strikes a note of caution:

> The aim of advertising is to improve the reputation of the client, not to improve the agency's reputation. And some clients are rightly worried when they see agencies more concerned about winning awards and getting applause than enhancing the reputation of the brand.

Of course, there is a certain obligation for advertising to be entertaining, for the simple reason that it guarantees higher audiences. For individual commercials, however, there is little evidence to connect high production values with high sales. Indeed, it is an old advertising chestnut that the advertisements that are the most effective are rarely the most creative or sophisticated – and are often the most irritating. It is worth noting that Procter & Gamble, who are notoriously professional in monitoring the value of advertising, have made only a minor concession to humour in their advertisements. Like many hard-liners, they still believe in 'Two Cs in a K' advertisements, in which two customers in a kitchen discuss the merits of a P&G product. As Simon Marquis, managing director of Burkitt Weinreich Bryant, sees it, 'The pendulum has perhaps swung too far away from the now unfashionable USP (unique selling proposition) to a point where tangible consumer benefits are apologetically buried in 30 seconds of televised bonhomie' (*Independent*, 6 March 1991, p.15).

THE GOLDEN RULE OF COMIC ADVERTISING

Making people laugh is tricky. Making them laugh while trying to sell them something is even more of a challenge, since the commercial can fall down on two grounds. On the one hand, the intended humour may simply not come off. It is almost impossible to cite culprits because the ripest examples are also the most forgettable. On the other hand, it is rarely sufficient for an advertiser simply to amuse its target audience in order to reap the sales benefits. There are many advertisements which do amuse but do not even begin to set the cash tills ringing. There are indications that, in substituting the hard sell for a more entertaining approach, some agencies have rather thrown out the baby with the bath water. All too often the product appears superfluous, a mere adjunct to the comic sketch.

For instance, there was a Volkswagen advertisement in which a couple are driving in a car down a deserted road. The woman is sleeping and there is a constant irritating squeak coming from some part of the car. Eventually, they stop at a petrol station and an old-timer comes out to assist them. He finally detects that the squeak is emanating from the woman's dangling earring. The old mechanic applies a little oil to it while she is still sleeping and sends them happily on their way. In this advertisement, the dramatic tension and comedy simply overshadowed the product impact. Anyone coming cold to the advertisement – without knowing the VW 'if only everything was as reliable' slogan – would surely not remember whether it was for a make of oil or a car. To understand the advertisement required familiarity, not just with the product but with the slogan. Arguably, over-sophistication had edged out the selling message. As Jeremy Bullmore saw the commercial, 'It was a sign that the agency was so wrapped up in 50 years of VW advertising that it assumed that the public was as conscious of it as they were.'

For a humorous advertisement to have real commercial impact, the product must be an integral part of the plot. Unless the humour is woven into the product message, the danger is that the jokes will merely serve to draw the attention away from the serious point. Used effectively, humour softens the sales blow and puts the audience in a relaxed and warm frame of mind, in which it is more attentive to what is being said. Ideally, the humour will serve as a means of subliminally, or painlessly, foisting the product benefits on to the viewer.

Clearly, humour should support an idea, not be the substitute for one. In much of today's advertising the story-line would still make sense if the product were removed. Establishing characters and comedy in commercials is one thing, but combining that with a positive product sell is more difficult. Jeremy Bullmore explained: 'Humour should be built-in not bolted-on. Once you've said that, you can sweep aside about three-quarters of humorous advertising, on that one criterion.'

He went on:

I think that the much-praised Holsten lager campaign, with Griff Rhys Jones, was a good example. You could take Holsten out of that and you'd still got a perfectly good all-purpose comic scenario. It wasn't singular to Holsten because even without the product, the ads still had a shape. You were left with quite an agreeable technique of interfacing a modern comedian with old movie footage, which is admirable and difficult and clever. But it was a generic campaign. More or less any product could have replaced it.

The humour in such commercials does not emerge from the nature of the product or the needs that it seeks to satisfy but is applied arbitrarily to it. The humour therefore fails to reveal anything of interest, importance or value about the product. For example, there was a series of Tennent's Pilsner spots which relied for their comic impact on a mixture of actions running forwards and backwards, including people jumping out of the sea and a water-skier towing a boat. The impression it left was one of a technique looking for a script. Advertisements in which the humour is not integrated may not bore, but neither are they likely to persuade. Lovable gloss is no substitute for real content and may raise doubts about the intrinsic value of the product.

A contrasting example was the campaign for Maxell tapes. In one commercial, a single protagonist stood in front of the camera listening to a 1960s hit, *The Israelites* by Desmond Decker. He nonchalantly tossed aside cards bearing the lyrics in time to the music, Bob Dylan fashion. The lyrics on his cards were nonsensical, but corresponded phonetically to the words in the song. For instance, the title was translated as 'Me ears are alight'. The last two cards read, 'I think that's what he said . . . But I need to hear it on a Maxell Tape.' Without the product the punchline makes no sense. The two become inseparably connected in the memory. Such advertisements set the product in the role of hero.

Opting for a humorous style of advertising, then, is fine provided it is not done at the expense of the selling principles on which advertising is founded. Advertising can be light-hearted but it must not stop there. The advertisement has to make the viewer think differently about a product or service. Advertising must always be a means to an end.

All this raises the question of whether humour running amok in advertising is a peculiarly British problem.

ANYONE FOR TEE-HEE?

Looking across the Channel to France, a rather different approach is apparent. Compared to Britain, the underlying tenor of French advertising is not amusing, but titillating. While the gratuitous use of sex is not alien to British advertising, it is almost *de rigueur* in France. As Liz Jensen wrote, 'Instead of being filled with ideas, French *pubs* (ads) are filled with bosoms. This tactic follows the great unspoken rule of French TV advertising – when in doubt, show a nice pair of *seins*' (*The Listener*, 22 December 1988, p.65).

So while British agencies will tend to look for a joke on which to hang their selling proposition, French agencies are on the look-out for a sexual hook. Not surprisingly, the French version of the Dunlopillo mattress advertisement discards the balancing-a-wineglass-on-it nonsense and gets straight to the heart of the matter: a couple on the mattress, doing what comes naturally. 'Dormez', runs the slogan, 'comme vous aimez'. Sex is dragged screaming into the unlikeliest commercials. There is a shoe advertisement which shows a wood at night where women are selling their charms. A man arrives and asks, 'How much . . .?' The women tell him the price of their shoes. And there are few advertisements for food that are not redolent with innuendo – ranging from the advertisement for ham in which the girl rolls a slice into a generous cylinder and inserts it between her parted lips (making our Cadbury's Flake offering look distinctly prissy) to the animated *crudités* which wriggle suggestively on a bed of lettuce in an advertisment for salad dressing. In French advertising, it seems, thirty seconds is ample time for a quickie.

This is not to suggest that Britain has some sort of monopoly on humorous advertising. Others, notably the Scandinavians and the Americans, are very adept at using humour to sell products. Rather, the difference is a qualitative one. British agencies are simply less constrained in their use of humour; the humour is more far-fetched, and fewer products are considered out of bounds.

Outside Britain, advertisers tend to use naturalistic settings for their commercials. Their scenarios obey the conventions of social realism. They create fictional situations which the audience can accept as reality.

The hallmark of British advertising is the proclivity for creating fantastic worlds. In these non-naturalistic settings the comic potential is far greater. Utterly implausible events are allowed to happen and even dominate proceedings. For instance, there was a classic Carling Black Label advertisement which recreated the Dambusters mission, and where a lone German sentry was invested with outstanding goalkeeping prowess which enabled him to 'save' the bouncing bombs and protect the dam.

Or again, consider the Sony campaign which featured John Cleese back in the early 1980s. The Sony management wanted to drop Cleese because it was felt he had been doing the job for too long and was overshadowing the product message. The company was keen to emphasize its technological leadership instead. A new campaign was devised, but during the testing phase the public indicated that they felt the new advertisements were not as good as the ones featuring Cleese. The agency concerned managed to reconcile the clash of interests in the domain of the unreal. It came up with a new campaign featuring a robot version of John Cleese, complete with bowler hat and silly walk, to emphasize the record of technological innovation.

Outside Britain, advertisers tend to steer clear of quirky scenarios, believing that they make for an unrealistic selling message. Simon Anholt of the multilingual copy-writing service, Translators in Advertising, explains: 'The British like humour, especially irony and puns. But you have to change this for the Germans and Swedes, who say that they don't buy from clowns' (*Independent*, 1 July 1992, p.17).

British advertisers have no such qualms about the persuasiveness of their selling message. As Michael Johnson, an American, and former editor of *International Management*, saw it:

In American commercials you'll find occasional humour but it's not as subtle or as pure as in Britain. The Americans will tend to mix a humorous message with a hard sell. You can't get away from an American commercial without getting clobbered on the head, whereas the British will, very subtly, leave you with a good feeling that you've just seen something witty – and as an afterthought, 'Oh yes, that was an advert for motor oil' or whatever.

A piece of research contrasting UK and US television commercials lends credence to this received wisdom. British agency executives credited humour with far more influence than did their American counterparts:

A more positive regard for humor in gaining attention, promoting comprehension, persuasion, gaining intention and enhancing source credibility is evident in the British responses. In particular, potential harmful effects of humor on recall and comprehension are of less concern to the British group.

(*Journal of Advertising*, 1989, p.41)

The research also showed that in Britain humour is considered a suitable treatment for a wider range of products (there were no taboo sectors), as well as a wider cross-section of consumers:

> While the U.S. executives see humor as best suited to younger, better-educated, male and upscale audiences, the British group was generally less biased towards these subgroups and more positive towards the use of humor with a wider array of audiences.
>
> (*Journal of Advertising*, 1989, p.41)

The evidence suggests that British agencies enjoy a kind of jokey complicity between copy-writer and consumer, that campaigns are admirably tailored to the British psyche. So where does this special relationship come from?

The British penchant for humour in advertising can be seen as the product of two critical factors. The first is that, traditionally, the British do not admire salesmanship in the way that Americans do. For instance, in Eric Kraft's novel *Herb 'n' Lorna* one of the characters is accepted into a new community on the strength of his salesmanship: 'but in a few months even the people who had resented him most when he arrived had to admit that Lester Piper was the best salesman they'd ever seen' (Kraft, 1989, p.121). That idea of salesmanship as a quality *per se* sits uneasily in the British context. Jeremy Bullmore comments:

> In Britain, there is a concern about salesmanship and selling. You don't say, 'This is the best tie in the world. I want you to buy it.' You try instead to involve people and to persuade them in an indirect, elliptical way.

BRITISH DIFFIDENCE TOWARD SELLING

In Britain, then, incorporating humour into the sales pitch has proved to be one of the more effective ways of tempering the uncomfortable process of selling and engaging the consumer. The British, after all, have always been suckers for a bit of humour – they invented the damned stuff. So British advertisers aim less for the hard sell and more for the padded sell.

The problem is that, having built up a tradition of making likeable commercials which has increasingly meant humorous ones, the public have come to expect commercials to amuse them, not to browbeat them. In cultivating this expectation, British advertising may have created a rod for its own back.

The second reason for the emphasis on humour is tied in with the way that British agencies carry out market research on new advertisements. Winston Fletcher explains:

> We tend to show new commercials in rough form to small groups of consumers. Unless they happen to be prospective purchasers, what they respond to is not whether the commercial is convincing, but whether it is enjoyable. The presumption is that if people enjoy your commercial they will feel better disposed towards your product; and if they dislike the commercial, they will feel ill-disposed towards the product. That is a dubious assumption, but it is widely held.

Ultimately, the bias towards humorous advertising goes beyond British consumers, or indeed the research methods, and extends to the advertisers and agencies. The decision-makers are educated people with sophisticated tastes. Their entourage, spouses, children and friends volubly tell them which commercials entertain them, as do editorial columns and awards juries. So, while they may try to be objective, it is understandable that they react favourably to those findings which they personally find believable and acceptable.

Humour turns out to be both the strength and the Achilles' heel of British advertising, and perhaps of British business as a whole.

Funny 7 Peculiar

Humour is possibly more of a national characteristic in Britain, not because of an inferiority complex, but through arrogance. Britain was an amazingly successful nation, and self-confidence enables you not to be too uptight. It meant we could laugh at ourselves. If anybody else laughed at us, we went to war with them. But I think that it's actually moved on in the last hundred years to become a nervous reaction to some of the cock-ups we've made.

(Sir Allen Sheppard, chairman, GrandMet)

Given that humour is a natural corollary to organizational life, what evidence is there that British managers are especially inclined to joke in and about business, and why should this be so?

WRY SOCIETY

Variously described as Britain's greatest natural asset, her finest invisible export and indispensable to her survival in 1940, the British sense of humour is credited with many things. It is that which simultaneously draws foreigners to her shores and provides them with a ready excuse for not laughing at British jokes.

Humour is regarded by the British as their own invention, if only because they were the first to give a name to the phenomenon. As far back as the sixteenth century, when other nations still used the

Latin word *humor* in a scientific context, the term had already infiltrated the popular language in Britain. As Frank Muir points out in his introduction to *The Oxford Book of Humorous Prose*:

> The French had their equivalents of 'comedy' and 'wit' and 'buffoonery' but their word *humeur* meant 'disposition' or 'mood'. The Germans, the Italians, the French all enjoyed upper-class wit and proletariat clowning but only the English, it seems, took pleasure in the middle area, in the recording of 'small but insignificant traits'. Wit was concerned with ideas and buffoonery with deeds, humour with people.
>
> (Muir, 1990, p.xxix)

Given that head start, Britain has gone on to exalt humour in a way other nations have not. Britain has dignified it with respectability and made a virtue out of it. As Theodore Zeldin wrote, 'England, alone in Europe, raised humour to the status of a trait of national character' (Zeldin, 1980, p.72).

In Britain, then, humour tends not to be so much action driven as personality driven. Having a sense of humour is considered a state of mind: it is personality-embedded. In France or Germany, say, it is about being witty, telling good jokes or being a raconteur; and in America it is about wisecracking and one-liners. British humour, as embodied in the better situation comedies, is character-based rather than gag-based; it is winsome rather than punchy. As David Nobbs, the creator of *The Fall and Rise of Reginald Perrin*, explained:

> I would like to think that it is the exploration of character and the interplay of characters that is our strength in Britain. What I write contains hardly any gags or wordplay — I regard those as too facile, not as mature as other kinds of humour.

It is not just the nature of British humour which sets it apart, but also its pervasiveness. Very few contexts are deemed inappropriate for humour. Indeed, where business is concerned, humour can be seen as the lubricant, jokers might say the driving force, behind British management.

WHERE OTHERS FEAR TO TREAD

America, like Britain, has a long and distinguished humorous tradition both in literature (from Mark Twain to Philip Roth) and on film (from Charlie Chaplin to Woody Allen). But unlike Britain, humour in America has something of a blind spot when crossed with business.

Anecdotal evidence of this can be seen in the nature of American situation comedies. While America boasts a string of excellent comedy shows in work settings like hospitals, law firms and police stations, business sitcoms are conspicuous by their absence. Of course, the same could be said of Britain (notwithstanding *Reginald Perrin*). The difference is that Britain does not tout its business organizations as the symbols and repositories of the nation's splendour and virtue.

So while Americans can joke about health, justice and crime, the corporate world remains strictly off-limits. It would seem that humour in America is constrained by the intensity of feeling surrounding organizational purpose. As Sir John Harvey-Jones saw it, 'In America they tend to take business more seriously – and a sense of humour tends to suggest you are not a deeply devoted corporate person.'

That sentiment was echoed by Sir Brian Wolfson: 'The Americans are more portentous about business, whereas Britain is still guided by the cult of the gifted amateur. Over here, business isn't so precious, nor so much in need of defence or respect.'

Further evidence of the sacrosanct nature of all things corporate can be seen in the American reaction to Winston Fletcher's humorous book, *Meetings, Meetings*. As Fletcher himself explains:

> I made it lighthearted to the degree that some people found it unpleasantly cynical. In America I had some really nasty reviews. I recall one review in Los Angeles which actually said that someone ought to collect all the copies of *Meetings, Meetings* and burn them.

While the reaction is extreme, it is by no means the only hint of religious zeal in American business. Management training videos are more emphatic still, with gurus such as Tom Peters holding forth like corporate evangelists. There is much ranting, waving of arms and gnashing of teeth. The high priests of success inject momentous phrases and biblical cadences into the virtues of enterprise and profit. The gurus know the only true path to corporate salvation. Follow them or be damned.

In contrast to this slick yet emotional appeal, what does Britain have? It has what are commonly referred to as 'John Cleese films'. Their aim is identical to those of the gurus. They are about popularizing and communicating good management practice. The gurus do this by anecdotalizing, by purging traditional management theory of its pretentious jargon and stuffiness; while Cleese and his cohorts do it by burlesquing the faults of disorganization and using high-quality comedy or drama to put the management lessons across. The success of these funny films comes from introducing what might be called the 'squirm factor' where viewers recognize themselves or colleagues in the portrayal. As Thomas Hobbes wrote some three centuries ago: 'Laughter is nothing else but sudden glory arising from some sudden conception of some eminency in ourselves, by comparison with the infirmity of others, or with our own formerly' (Hobbes, 1650).

This approach is deemed particularly appropriate in Britain. Tina Tietjen, head of Video Arts, explains:

> The fact that the British don't mind sending themselves up makes it possible to use the 'wrong-way, right-way' format. In Britain, there is a much readier acceptance of fallibility, than perhaps in the US. Americans are still very hung up about the idea that they should never discuss doing anything wrong; they should only talk about doing things the right way. There is limited humour in the 'right way'. Real fun comes from the silliness of the wrong-way.

Once again, humour is seen to come from incongruity. There is little humour in efficiency since that is what business is about. There is no tension. Humour in the corporate context resides in spectacular or eccentric displays of inefficiency and fallibility. And that is precisely what the British market wants, as revealed by management writer and advertising agency chairman Winston Fletcher:

> When I went to my publisher with the idea for a book called Superefficiency, he said make it lighthearted like Meetings, Meetings. Unfortunately, I couldn't see a way of saying to people, 'You should

organize your own lives, ha ha.' Nobody thinks that it's funny to be efficient. They think it's funny to be inefficient.

THE DEFECTIVE EXECUTIVE

"Goodnight, Miss Travis.
I've finished my coffee but I've left my biscuit.
Put it in my in-tray and I'll deal with it tomorrow."

The capacity of British managers to laugh at themselves is not confined to the training experience. It comes through in real life too. In Britain, efficiency, productivity and profit are constant targets for wisecracks, often self-deprecating ones: 'increase productivity by 5 per cent? You've really got to stop smoking that stuff.' Or take the observation of a personnel manager charged with implementing a redundancy programme: 'Apparently, the quickest way to create a small business in this country is to start with a big business.' And consider the production director who dismisses the suggestion that the firm should manufacture rather than buy in a simple component with: 'Let's stick to what we're good at . . . losing vast sums of money.' Such irreverence from American lips is unthinkable to the point of blasphemy.

Humour in business is an un-American activity. Business should not be sent up, nor businessmen ridiculed because both embody that fragile thing that is the American heritage. In the absence of a collective heritage, Americans have invested heavily in a set of political and economic values embedded in individual liberty and economic opportunity.

This is not to say that Americans do not joke in their organizations. On the contrary, they use humour extensively on formal and informal occasions. Jokes are invariably used to warm up speeches and presentations, but once they 'get down to business' humour is unlikely to intrude on proceedings. Indeed, subsequent attempts at humour may be met with stunned silence. And while American business humour can range from the robust to the refined, jibes will steer clear of the company's products or the importance of 'the bottom line'. A playful comment like, 'Perhaps it's time to give up the idea of profit as a motive' is unlikely to raise a smile in America.

The American corporate environment is also very litigious which further constrains the use of humour in business. American managers are terrified of lawsuits. Anyone with a grievance can find a lawyer to represent them. Age, sex and race discrimination cases proliferate. Thus managers have to be more direct in evaluating their subordinates' performance. Any criticism has to be clear and unambiguous, or managers run the risk of being sued for unfair dismissal. Humour, with its scope for misinterpretation, becomes a liability rather than an asset.

Take the example of the British management team discussing how and when they should announce someone's forthcoming redundancy. It is mid-December, and one of the managers suggest they insert it as a riddle in his Christmas cracker: 'Guess who doesn't work for the company anymore?' Such flippancy would be misplaced in a culture where executives can wind up in court for making off-colour remarks – though corporate America gets its own back by leading the world in the output of jokes against lawyers.

American selectivity with regard to humour is not unique. Managers in other countries also place limits on the extent to which they allow humour to intrude on business. For instance, French managers do not usually spice up their presentations with humour. If they do, their humour is more likely to be clever and sophisticated, a glimpse of their intellectual brawn, not their playfulness. The risk of appearing foolish, with the accompanying loss of personal dignity and intellectual standing, tends to inhibit access to other forms of humour.

Similarly, in meetings, even relatively informal ones, humour is rarely used with intent, to drive home a point or defuse tension. That would be seen as frivolous. Yet French restraint has little to do with the American tendency to place the corporation's role in society on a pedestal. On the contrary, in France business or money are treated with healthy disrespect, even cynicism, outside the office. But at work there is an emphasis on keeping up appearances, on being *sérieux*: that is, both conscientious and credible.

That interpersonal restraint at work is reinforced linguistically by the predominance of the polite *vous* form of address. Even managers who have worked together for years may choose not to adopt the more familiar *tu* form of address. This inevitably creates a linguistic barrier to the sort of psychological intimacy required by humour, with its attendant self-revelation. The personal remarks and needling which are so much a part of British office life would be considered intrusive and rude.

German managers too do not see levity as belonging to the workplace. In some countries promotion is accompanied by a certain 'loosening up'. But in Germany the reverse is more likely to be the case. With seniority comes responsibility and the incumbent must be seen to deserve it and take it seriously.

Joking is fine outside work and amongst friends. At work, it is important to focus on the tasks or problems in hand and humour is deemed to distract from that. To a greater extent than even the French, Germans compartmentalize humour. The more formal the occasion, the less humour is acceptable.

Humour would be allowed only in so far as it contributes to the *Arbeitsklima* (working environment) and supports the high task orientation which characterizes many German companies. For the same reason, what little tactical joking there is in the workplace is likely to be aimed at ineptitude and nonconformity and can be quite caustic. The jokey warning to one latecomer, 'There'll be a note in your personnel file', is indicative of the style. But humour is never self-deprecating since that might suggest inadequacy and would be at odds with the emphasis placed on personal competence.

So other national business cultures tend to place restrictions either on the nature of the humour or on its targets. Recourse to humour is regulated. In Britain, on the other hand, the aversion is to seriousness. Something guaranteed to make British eyes glaze over is a phrase such as, 'We're very excited about the new management control system.' As John Mole wrote of British business, 'Humour is expected at all levels, between all levels, and on all occasions. It is important to be entertaining on every possible occasion, public or private' (Mole, 1990, p.111).

Thus, while French managers are concerned to show their

intellectual panache during meetings, Germans will want to demonstrate their serious-minded command of the business in hand, and Americans will seek to busy themselves (create tasks and fix deadlines). Meanwhile their British counterparts are on the look-out for openings in which to squirt humour. For instance, when an administration manager reports that there are fundamental problems in the typing pool, one of his colleagues chips in, 'the one-armed secretary, for a start'. When another manager claims that he is not one to fob off inept staff on to other departments, one of his colleagues mimes an elongating Pinocchio nose for the benefit of the others present. Or again, a shrewd suggestion on the part of one manager prompts a colleague's admiration, 'Excellent idea. Shame it was yours.' Mock rivalry is also apparent when one manager volunteers his colleague for an unpleasant task and the latter threatens, 'I'll get you in the playground.' Britons often view business meetings as an exercise in competitive joking.

This is worth bearing in mind, both for Britons doing business abroad and for foreign executives coming to Britain. Guidebooks offering tips to travelling British executives make a point of reminding them to retain their sense of humour. This is seen as a foil to the frustration they will experience with bureaucratic rigmarole and obstructive, non-English speaking locals. But the advice does not necessarily extend to actual dealings with foreign counterparts.

Although humour can establish an immediate rapport, the dangers of humour backfiring are increased when the two parties do not share a common culture. British managers can easily cause offence or confusion by the inappropriate use of humour. Irony and sarcasm are particularly risky since they may be taken rather literally. It is therefore probably wise to show humorous restraint, at least until the parties have achieved a certain familiarity. Sir Brian Wolfson offers a salutary warning:

> A couple of years ago a few of us were speaking at an international management conference in Portugal with simultaneous translation. I decided to be funny and I died an absolute death. There wasn't a smile or a flicker except from three of my pals who cracked up completely, not at the jokes, but at the effect they weren't having on the audience.

The lesson is reversible for foreigners on assignments in Britain. With the British sense of humour being so quirky, it is probably wiser for foreigners to ingratiate themselves by showing an appreciation for it, rather than by trying to emulate it.

The high esteem in which British managers hold humour is further reflected in their choice of managerial role models. The brand of individualism that Britons look for in their leaders is more likely to be based on eccentricity and nonconformity than no-nonsense self-reliance in the American sense. It follows that the mantle occupied by straight-talking Lee Iacocca in America was filled in Britain by ebullient Sir John Harvey-Jones, 'an avuncular, ho-ho-ho 68-year-old with long, unkempt hair and a taste for wearing ties that belong in other men's bottom drawers' (*Independent on Sunday*, 6 December 1992, p.23).

NAUGHTY KNIGHT

Perhaps the closest the British public has come to seeing a top manager in action has been the *Troubleshooter* series, in which Sir John Harvey-Jones visited ailing British companies. The programmes provided a unique insight into the singularities of the British management style. In particular, Sir John demonstrated the extent to which British managers have recourse to humour and laughter to get information and to deliver painful criticism.

A simple question like 'Who is responsible for maximizing the profit from the factory?' had the management of a toy firm reaching for the cyanide pills. After a couple of goes at answering, each greeted by a chuckle from the affable knight, they gave up. Sir John was charming but devastating.

Indeed, there were times when his laughter said more than his words. For instance, on hearing about a firm's pitifully low design budget and that they were intending to go up-market, he commented incredulously, 'Well it would be difficult not to go up-market from that!' and launched into an infectious, high-pitched giggle.

Humorous backhanders were his speciality. At the Morgan sports car firm he confided, 'I can't see what's stopping your profit going up, except a touching diffidence and lack of greed on your part.' Later he pointed out that 'Some of the lathes you've got, I haven't seen since I was a bloody boy.' Or again, on being shown round the chaotic factory floor, his guide intoned, 'The layout is historic.' 'I'd assumed,' answered Sir John wryly.

He also showed a quirky turn of phrase, saying on one occasion,

'Sometimes in business you have to kill your favourite child to succeed.' And he was capable of mixing his metaphors for comic effect: 'The sausage machine has got you by the balls,' he told one of the Roper brothers at Churchill Tableware. His use of the jovial aphorism made the advice more palatable. For instance, he told the management at Morgan, 'You may as well go for more radical change because . . . you only get shot once.'

Perhaps his most powerful use of humour was when it came to meeting new people. One chairman was immediately put at ease with Harvey-Jones's self-mocking 'It must feel like the coming of the Lord.' And he was equally at home with people on the shop-floor. Barriers of resistance or apprehension were quickly disman-tled with a joke or throw-away line. He would marvel at their skill. One woman who was counting and stamping plates was greeted with, 'Well that's the first time I've ever felt sorry for a machine.' There was immediate empathy. Here was real-life proof that Victor Borge got it right when he defined humour as 'the shortest distance between two people'. Employees volunteered information to Harvey-Jones on camera which their own bosses could not have extracted from them with electrodes.

His mastery of gentle teasing, irony and contemptuous humour as well as his sensitivity to situations were exemplary. He was equally adept at using humour to scold, to befriend and to goad into action. People were gently steered towards his point of view. Sensibilities were spared. Sir John himself described his management style as 'lovable': 'Basically I try to jolly things along' (*Independent on Sunday*, 11 March 1990, p.26).

The ease and frequency with which Harvey-Jones slipped in and out of the humorous mode was central to his personal style, but it also told us a lot about what Britons look for in a leader.

THE LIGHT BRIGADE

Profiles of business leaders in the British quality press almost invariably allude to the individual's sense of humour, if only to say that it failed to put in an appearance. In much the same way as the Eskimo vocabulary is replete with words for snow, so Britons show nuance in their descriptions of humour. Consider a random selection from recent business profiles in *The Times*. Managers were variously described as having a sense of humour which was 'sardonic', 'impish', 'puckish', 'mordant', 'irrepressible', 'sharp', 'rakish', 'rapier-like', 'wry', 'ruggerish', 'deadpan' and 'wicked'. With a single adjective to go on, Britons are able to summon up a whole personality.

A person's sense of humour is a vital *point de repère* in Britain. It is how Britons situate people. Just as the French are interested in educational credentials or Americans look for evidence of personal drive (often measured by salary), so Britons want to know about the sense of humour. It transpires that having a sense of humour and knowing how to deploy it is considered advantageous for British leaders. This does not mean that every British leader has one. What it does mean is that those who are deficient are considered to have a chink in their armour (the only public figure exempt from this expectation being the sovereign, in whom its public suppression is proof of absolute self-denial and commitment to service). In Britain, humour is most conspicuous when it is absent, in the same way as a lack of drive or optimism would seem amiss in America.

Given this national obsession with humour, one can well understand that British managers are at pains to avoid being dubbed humourless. If they cannot crack a joke, they may go out of their way to show that they take one. In many countries the attendant loss of face would be seen as undermining managerial authority. But in Britain it is the refusal to 'go along with the joke' which is more likely to damage a person's authority. To be accused of not having a sense of humour is tantamount to being stripped of one's birthright. British males in particular are more likely to own up to being poor drivers or lovers than to admit a deficiency in the humour department.

A vivid demonstration of that burden can be seen among high-profile British politicians. There is, it seems, a shared determination among the victims of modern British satire to put a brave face on their discomfiture; to express feelings of fondness even for the malevolent marionettes on *Spitting Image*.

For example, the programme's portrayal of Sir David Steel in Dr Owen's pocket, crooning 'Oh David' adoringly, almost certainly damaged the Alliance's chances in the 1987 election. Yet Sir David harboured no grudges: 'It didn't upset me. It was part of the game.' Or again, consider Roy Hattersley's proud reaction to his squelchy-voiced puppet: 'I'm the eponymous hero. I'm the only one who actually spits' (*The Listener*, 26 April 1990, p.12). Even Kenneth Baker went on record as saying that he did not mind being depicted as a slug. However much we suspect the true feelings of those lampooned, we cannot help but admire their willingness to grin and bear it.

HOW BRITISH BOSSES WISH TO BE REMEMBERED

"I hear he was something of a practical joker."

This raises the more complex question: why is humour relevant to the way business is done in Britain? There are two answers: first, humour in business is simply a spill-over from certain features of British society; and second, humour is a force which helps to reconcile the needs of business with the values of British society.

PLAY ON WORDS

The most obvious place to look for an explanation of national variations in management style is in the language. The English language, with its nuance and flexibility, makes it easy for British managers to engage in humour.

Britain's richest heritage is not artistic, musical or philosophical, but literary, the most obvious flowering being the works of William Shakespeare. This shared legacy provides a high level of subliminal understanding and a wealth of common references on which to draw. It is not uncommon, for instance, to hear managers, consciously or otherwise, quoting the Bard for comic effect. Take the head of marketing who reckons that the slashed advertising budget is the 'unkindest cut of all'; or the sales manager who refers to one salesman as having 'no stomach for the fight'; or even the distribution manager who complains that a wronged client 'doesn't want his pound of flesh; he wants a whole bloody abattoir.' English literature is replete with quotations that can be reworked or parodied, and which are familiar to most educated people.

Sometimes just a snatch is enough, as in the case of the head of department, surrounded by computer printouts but unable to find a sheet of writing paper: 'paper, paper everywhere . . .' he mutters, invoking 'The Rime of the Ancient Mariner' and letting his voice trail off. His secretary smiles in sympathy, thus demonstrating that she knows what is implied and agrees with it.

Shakespeare's all-purpose phrases have passed into the popular consciousness. They are part of our conversational furniture and are easily reworked or given a topical twist. When we say, with a wry smile, 'As luck would have it . . .' how many of us would realize we were quoting from *The Merry Wives of Windsor*? Yet the majority of Britons would recognize the conspiratorial hint in that remark. This breadth of vocabulary leads to nuance of expression. Jeremy Bullmore pointed out, 'The more words you have in your repertoire, the funnier you can be. It would be difficult to express subtle differences of meaning in Esperanto.'

Compared to managers in other English-speaking countries, Britons tend to be less explicit or direct. There is something of the club exchange in much of their managerial communication. They will 'put out feelers'. People will be 'sounded out' in a very British way. Sir Peter Parker saw British linguistic empathy thus:

We're islanders. We have all those closed short-hand things. There is that familiarity and closeness which breeds an idiom. We feel comfortable putting complicated things simply. It's part of the style, part of British education that you can, under very difficult situations, pull everything together, to catch a whole network of implications in a pithy phrase. We can say very briefly, 'I've had it' — and with that you're saying something colossal.

This idea of a shared code was exemplified by Richard Branson's warning to a colleague: 'Look Trevor, I like these people and I think that they want to do a deal. But we shouldn't sign anything, unless we can live with it' (*Financial Times*, 14 February 1992, p.10).

Britain, then, is a high-context culture. It takes time to become conversant with the subtleties. It is not only what is said that counts, but how it is said, who said it and when. The language is firmly rooted in the features of tone, gesture and expression. So when a British boss says that 'it might be worth looking into' a problem, one has to decipher whether the implication is 'when you get a chance' or 'jump to it!' What is behind the words is as important as the words themselves. In a low-context culture, such as North America, the bulk of information, intentions and meanings are conveyed in words and sentences. Similarly, when a German manager says that an idea is interesting, he or she actually means it. But when a British manager says it, the other party has to deduce from the way it is said whether that constitutes approval or dismissal. Sir John Harvey-Jones pointed out: 'In Britain we tend to convey as much by what is left unsaid – by the pauses, the silence and the tone – as by what is actually said.'

By Euro-American standards, communication in Britain is less direct and more suggestive. This gives British managers a head start over their foreign counterparts when it comes to using humour, since implicitness is one of its requirements. An explicit joke is either not explicit or not a joke.

To add to this depth and nuance of vocabulary there is a tendency in Britain to understate, to 'curve' the language, to eschew the direct in favour of the pithy or the elliptical. For instance, Britons are much given to using metaphors and similes to express their views in a whimsical manner.

Winston Fletcher used imagery to try to convey the difficulties of managing an advertising agency. 'Trying to manage creatives', he explained, 'is like trying to herd cats.' Such analogies are powerful stimuli. As listeners, we become part-authors of these images as we re-create them in our heads.

Former Burton chairman Ralph Halpern was once told by his advertising director, Richard Birtchnell: 'But Ralph, if you don't decide to do this now, we're going to miss the boat.' His reply was, 'I don't mind missing the boat if it's the Titanic' (*GQ*, June 1991, p.119). Halpern thus killed two birds with one stone, quashing the implication that he was indecisive and ridiculing the impulsiveness of his colleague.

Or consider the middle manager in an insurance company who was getting fed up with having reams of paper printed out by his subordinates simply because they 'did not trust the system'. He warned them, 'If you don't stop it, I'm going to come and give your printer a vasectomy.'

Another example is the training manager of one beleaguered company whose training budget had just been halved. In terms of trying to put the company back on its feet, he explained, this was 'like feeding a starving man on diet biscuits'. Once again, the use of analogy left an indelible image.

An alternative way of making an impact is to summon up a mental caricature. The regional director of a construction company used this approach to get his point across. He was telling his site manager that the proposed project did not warrant two storemen being employed and concluded: 'We're not going to pay a bloke to spend 90 per cent of the day with his feet up reading Enid Blyton books.'

Later in the same meeting, he painted another humorous scenario to try to persuade the project team to find an alternative to security guards patrolling the site: 'A pimply lad in a uniform with a walkie-talkie isn't going to deter anyone. It'll be like high season at the superstore.'

The ease with which British managers make humorous allusions reflects, and breeds, a tolerance for ambiguity.

VAGUELY AMUSING

Britons are comfortable with ambiguity. Again, this is rooted in the admirable vagueness of the language. No language seems better suited to the framing of open-ended questions or projective try-ons. Its apotheosis is perhaps the word 'like'. A vague enquiry such as, 'What's so-and-so like?' will often prompt a reply that is sharp, witty, succinct, in a language that the participants share: something along the lines, 'a bit half-soaked', 'all right in small doses', or 'not bad for a paper weight'.

Ambiguity shows up in other ways too. Britain has no written constitution, no Bill of Rights or legal code. Political and legal systems are based on precedent, inference, compromise and negotiation. Similarly, in business, the British have an aversion to working within a rational and systematic framework. Consider the British system of industrial relations. Unlike, say, German or Swedish companies, British companies do not have an institutional-ized system of industrial democracy.

Britons take pride in 'getting there in the end', in finding the expedient solution rather than the cleverest solution. They are not keen on trying to take out uncertainty by planning, procedures and control. The systemization of American management with its

standard operating procedures governing everything from personnel to purchasing does not suit the British, who like room to
manoeuvre, zones of discretion, and hidden rules to identify club
members.

British managers, then, do not want issues publicly resolved,
thereby creating a precedent which has to be respected. They can
work without everything being explicit. They can transact in terms
of nods and winks and body language. Things get done in notes,
telephone calls, a word at lunch. Conversation is typically imprecise
and vague, full of hints and subtleties. Contrasting British managers
with their foreign counterparts, John Mole observed, 'Facts and
figures and definitive statements are avoided, as is direct confrontation and argument. For outsiders used to clarity, decisiveness and
demonstrative professionalism this can be misleading' (Mole, 1990,
p.110).

This British fondness for fudging and ambiguity finds a natural
ally in humour. Humour is a way of delivering criticism with a smile,
of singling out bad behaviour while confirming a sense of belonging,
of challenging authority without appearing to do so.

Another reason that British managers yield easily to humour is
because of the quasi-obligation not to take anything, especially
oneself, too seriously.

THE WIT PARADE

The British knack for making light of serious things (the 'just a flesh
wound' school of bravery) and for taking trivial matters seriously
(cricket, *par excellence*) is a legacy of aristocratic values. In Britain,
ruling-class manners and mores have been accepted, at least as an
ideal, by a wider social constituency. As Anthony Cooper, Third
Earl of Shaftesbury, put it:

> 'Twas the saying of an ancient sage, that humour was the only test of
> gravity; and gravity, of humour. For a subject which would not bear
> raillery was suspicious; and a jest which would not bear serious
> examination was certainly false wit.
>
> (Cooper, 1709, p.5)

Business is no exception. Britons do not treat business with anything like the same deference as other nations: first, because it is

not quite seen as worthy of a person's undivided time and attention; and second, because there is no perceived conflict between engaging in humour and 'taking care of business'. For instance, when one departmental manager revealed the proposed restructuring of the division to his deputy, he added: 'It's not for briefing. Just read it and eat it.' Similarly, two colleagues are berating their boss's lack of enterprise: 'He drags like an anchor on the team's initiative,' says one. The other queries, 'Is that anchor with a "W"?'

The routine alternation between the serious and the comical seems accentuated in Britain. It was noted by Michael Johnson, an expatriate American:

> One often encounters an interesting schizophrenia in British managers. They can be incredibly funny, and loose, and animated in a very witty way for five minutes and then instantly switch to a very serious demeanour, which I personally find a little disconcerting.

This easy shift between modes derives, in part, from the weak partition in Britain between work and leisure. Work is seen as a re-enactment of real life, not some pale imitation of it. Ralf Dahrendorf, former head of the London School of Economics, wrote, 'Work is about life, not life about work. Britain's version of liberty is living at work rather than just living for work' (Dahrendorf, 1982, p.46).

It follows from the British view of work as an extension of life that humour should bring colour to the workplace just as it does outside. If humour did not carry over into business life, the latter would appear untypical and incomplete. Why should managers leave their sense of humour behind when they go into the office? As Sir Brian Wolfson confirmed:

> I like working in an atmosphere where humour prevails — not dominates, otherwise it would be a variety show — and there is a serious job to do. But either in life and in work — and, to me, work's just a microcosm of life — there is room for laughter.

Nor is humour among British managers inhibited by a strong sense of personal dignity as it is, say, among the Italians, the Germans or the French. There is, in the British character, a certain shameless-ness, of the knotted-hanky-on-the-beach variety. Britons have many hang-ups, but a sense of humour is one of the few things that they can legitimately flaunt. It is this which, in the past, has allowed thousands of managers and bosses to go into work sporting a red nose for charity on Comic Relief Day. One can ill imagine continental managers engaging in such bouts of minor comic exhibitionism – though, as Miles Kington once pointed out, the British need a Comic Relief Day about as much as the Germans need a Special Efficiency Day, or the French need an Intellectual Argument Day.

NO EFFORT SPARED

"April fool, Miss Henstooth!"

It follows that British managers are uniquely inclined towards self-deprecation as a form of humour. A British businessman is quite capable of joking that he is 'thankful for the thirty-year lunch break which has been my career'. Why? Because he takes both the pursuit of business excellence and his own professionalism with a pinch of salt. Or consider the middle manager who was greeted by his boss with 'You're in early this morning.' Instead of grasping the opportunity to stress his commitment to his work, the manager snapped into music hall mode, 'You'd come in early if you slept with my wife.' In the British scheme of things, comments are first scanned for humorous cues before receiving a straight answer. Everyone plays stooge to everyone else.

British managers who joke in this way are not undermining their credibility. They are more likely to be enhancing it, for humour, as a byword for charisma, social skills and persuasiveness, is what Britons feel management is all about. Humour upholds one's right to manage in Britain as might displays of intellectual flourish in France, or technical grasp in Germany. Humour also suggests a certain improvisational skill which is admired in British life and management.

DROLLNESS IN THE DOLDRUMS

Britain does not have a culture of reliability. The proper functioning of services and material infrastructure cannot be counted upon. Britons are brought up to expect the unexpected or, more accurately, not to expect the expected. Public transport is perhaps the most blatant example of disorganization and contempt for customer service. Travellers have to incorporate possible timetable errors or transport delays on their own schedules. And the same ethos taints the corporate environment.

In companies of all sizes, promises may be greeted with scepticism, prompt responses with surprise, and errors with resignation. Britain has had a poor service ethic and poor quality and delivery records: the upshot is that nothing can be taken for granted. Managers earn corporate Brownie points for 'making the best of a bad job'. Jocular cynicism and off-the-cuff resourcefulness provide the best means of combating unpredictability and living with underachievement. Never mind the quality, feel the wit.

Related to that uncertainty of outcome is a wider scepticism about governing one's own destiny. It is pointless to try to take control, improper to get too involved, arrogant to attempt to outwit fate. It is enough just to be. This too, is an attitude which carries over into the business environment, and which explains the relative British indifference towards American accounts of spectacular business turn rounds of the 'in one mighty bound Jack was free' variety.

Britons do not share the American belief that anything is possible encapsulated in the American clichéd insult, 'Get a life!' Business success in Britain is sometimes regarded as rather a hit-or-miss affair. Many British managers subscribe to the view that they are as likely to do the right thing for the wrong reasons as the wrong thing for the right reasons. The outcome of any managerial decision is seen as something of a lottery, and the manager as a sometime hapless victim of turbulent economic forces.

Here again, humour provides an antidote. In America when things go awry they say, 'I gave it my best shot'. In Britain when all else fails, 'we still have our sense of humour'. It is the one thing that even the Japanese cannot take away.

STIFF UPPER QUIPS

Britain's culture of unreliability ties in with a peculiar affection for the humour that resides in the shortfall between aspiration and achievement. The idea of humour as an expression of dignity in defeat has always struck a chord in the British consciousness. There is nobility in struggling gamely against adversity. It is not just losing but how you lose that counts. The culture of failure is enshrined in Stephen Pile's anthology of *Heroic Failures* (1980), which achieved bestseller status. Another manifestation was the advertisement which accompanied England's exit from the 1990 World Cup: it featured Bobby Robson, the England football manager, posing with a wan smile and a glowing panatella. Underneath the photo was the caption: 'Happiness is a cigar called Hamlet.' One doubts whether the manager of any other national team would have co-operated with such an advertisement – or whether the theme of laughing through adversity, which has sustained Hamlet's advertising since 1964, could have worked elsewhere.

There is something in the national psyche which prompts Britons to purge themselves of conspicuous underachievement by shouting it from the roof-tops rather than discreetly sweeping it under the carpet. Populist politicians invoke the spirit of Dunkirk far more readily than the spirit of 'victories' such as El Alamein. Crowing in victory seems indecent; but shared suffering, nobly overcome, can be celebrated without embarrassment. As Sir John Harvey-Jones saw it, 'It is particularly British to laugh at ourselves especially when things get really bad. That is when laughter really comes into its own.'

Perhaps it has something to do with Britain's past greatness. The tensions between former glory and present condition give special poignancy to cracks about being on the crest of a slump, especially in business, where humour serves as an adjustment to long-term decline and economic under-performance. Humour transforms business calamity into occupational therapy. And on an individual level almost any bad experience carries with it the consolation of an anecdote in the making. Even as disaster strikes, British managers are thinking how best to relate it to their colleagues. They wipe the flaw with humour.

The form of humour which best demonstrates one's 'stiff upper lip' is understatement. This fulfils the dual purpose of suggesting nonchalant wit and projecting an impression of coolness and insouciance. Comic effect is regularly derived in Britain by creating a state of tension between the gravity of the observed and the way it is rated. For instance, Terry Waite, the former hostage, explained how his captors beat him violently on the soles of his feet, summing up the experience as 'painful – not to be recommended!' (*Guardian*, 23 December, 1991 p.2). And there was the case of General Sir Anthony Farrar-Hockley, a former army commander in Northern Ireland, who found a suspicious object in his garden hose-pipe. When asked by television interviewers what he thought of the whole incident, he replied with a smile, 'I don't care for people leaving explosive devices in my garden' (BBC 1 *News*, 13 August, 1990). Or again, consider the reaction of a diner in the Carlton Club when it was bombed by terrorists in June 1990: 'I thought to myself: "This is no mishap in the kitchen." ' (*Independent*, 30 June, 1990, p.16).

UNDER THE TOP

"Oh, not bad . . . how are things with you?"

These examples from public life are replicated in the boardroom and on the shop-floor: personal blunders are typically greeted with, 'This could take some explaining,' while full-blown catastrophes may prompt the admission that 'Things don't look too good'. This is not to say that exaggeration does not have its place in British humour. It is simply that, confronted with a very thin man, Britons are more likely to suggest that he is 'not exactly overweight' than to depict him as a 'matchstick man'. It is one more element of the British 'code' which foreigners have to crack.

Evidently, the idea advanced in Chapter 4 that humour is a way for individuals to handle uncertainty and failure can be extended to Britain as a nation. But humour serves as a mitigating factor in other ways too.

FIT FOR BUSINESS

Business is embedded in society. A nation's values impinge heavily on the prevailing management style. For instance, it is sometimes said of the Americans that they are always selling something. Their confrontational, lapel-grabbing management style mirrors their skill at self-promotion, their direct interpersonal approach. Their business energy reflects their everyday optimism. Britain, on the other hand, is less in tune with the ethos of business.

In Britain, the fit between business and society is not as snug as it is in America. Many of the features associated with 'good business practice' – candour, assertiveness, tenacity, professionalism, manipulation, money-orientation and so on – are not valued by British society. In Britain, it is important on a social level to be a 'nice person'; that is, courteous, unassuming and unabrasive. Self-deprecation and false humility are more appreciated than self-assertion. It was this which prompted Prime Minister John Major to comment: 'Modesty may be an attractive quality. But as a nation we carry it too far' (*Independent*, 21 November 1992, p.18).

Thus the tensions already existing in business are amplified in the British context – and there is a correspondingly greater need for humour to mitigate these tensions. In particular, humour serves as a smoke-screen for greed, ambition and conflict.

For instance, in comparison with America, British society is inhospitable to the idea of money-making. The single-minded pursuit of hard cash is deemed to erode the human spirit. It is considered distasteful to haggle over a fee or any matter concerning money. British managers are loathe to tell colleagues how much they earn, and they certainly do not admire money openly in the American fashion. Yet there are times when matters of finance do need to be discussed candidly, and this is where humour intervenes.

Humour allows Britons to feign detachment. In America, it is perfectly all right to be serious about business and finance because they are considered laudable pursuits. Not so in Britain, where integrity is preserved by pretending it is all a bit of a game, or by referring dismissively to the 'sordid subject of the coin'.

Humour is also used to affect indifference towards ambition. Britons in every walk of life are at pains to keep their personal ambition from public view. The British public despises those who are 'obviously on the make', the key word being *obviously*. Britons are wary of driving ambition. Thus power is accepted rather than pursued. Even in politics, candidates do not *decide* to stand for the party leadership but have to be *urged* to do so and, with visible reluctance, they will 'let their names go forward' or 'throw their hats into the ring'. Britons prefer to have greatness thrust upon them.

That same diffidence applies in business. Humour will be used to deflect direct questions about ambition. So, when asked whether he would like his boss's job, one middle manager reels off a series of pros and cons, then dismisses the idea: 'Anyhow, I would have to learn to play golf.' Similarly, when a senior executive asked a former colleague whether he had yet been made director, the latter responded, 'No, I'm still an honest man.' Humour is used as a cover for thwarted ambition as well as for future aspirations.

The idea that gentlemen should not be *seen* to be striving is one which harks back to the tradition of the gifted amateur. It is consistent with the British view of achievement which, if it is to be of any value, should appear effortless. Success, unless fluky, can look grubby and gauche. There is a distaste for excess or assertion. There is a preference for instinct over logic, and character over intelligence. Displays of personal efficiency or smartness will often attract contempt rather than praise. Remarks such as 'How very clever of you' or 'That's jolly efficient of you' are rarely meant as compliments. George Mikes, a keen observer of the English character, wrote:

In England it is bad manners to be clever, to assert something confidently. It may be your personal view that two and two make four, but you must not state it in a self-assured way, because this is a democratic country, and others may be of a different opinion.

(Mikes, 1946, p.36)

In Britain, it is bad form to be sure of your authority or expertise. It is all right to have authority but it should be carried lightly. As Sir Brian Wolfson saw it:

> I don't know of anybody in commerce, industry or politics who's had real power, who isn't to some extent changed — and I think that the mitigating factor against appalling or disproportionate change is whether they have humour. As I see it, a strong sense of humour, and particularly a self-deprecating one, is the strongest single antidote to power corrupting.

For example, the general manager of a luxury London hotel described his job thus:

> At social gatherings I sometimes get asked what I do, and I say, 'I'm a hotel manager.' Generally, people then insult me by saying, 'Oh, have you been doing that long?' as though it were the kind of job anybody could do. The trouble is, they are probably right!

The tag line is typically British. It is self-deprecating and deliberately softens what might have been interpreted as delusions of grandeur.

In the British scheme of things, then, a lack of humour is equated with a lack of humanity. Achievement must be tempered with a sense of social responsibility. British managers are expected to show restraint with the power they wield, and even to acknowledge, in a jokey way, the odd personal flaw. They have been brought up to believe that those in command can afford to underplay their hands. It is important not to lose the 'common touch'. The idea is to get one's way by putting people at their ease, not by beating them into submission with arguments or authority. British managers prefer to sidle up and coax rather than to confront.

HUMOURING PEOPLE

British society is not confrontational. Britons are shocked by foreigners who have the temerity to complain about the service in restaurants. In spite of the upsurge in service expectations, people in Britain still do not like to 'make a fuss' or 'create a scene'. Take the example of an aggrieved policy-holder writing a letter of complaint to his insurance company:

Dear Sirs

I've spoken to Nicola – Alan Robinson's PA
Who said I must tell you what I've got to say.
I've been paying my policies – admittedly by cheque
Your reaction has been 'Good Grief' and 'Oh Heck'
'We don't want your money unless it's DD'
And you're going to return my cheques to me!

The problem I've got is simple enough
I've an erratic supply of the folding stuff.
I can't guarantee when my payments are due
That my bank will send the money to you.
If my balance is down on the day you request it
I'll get stung by the bank – I don't want to test it.

I never thought it would come to pass
That a company would ever refuse my brass
But rules can be waived, I'm sure you'll agree
So for a short time persevere with me
When my problems begin to abate
I'll gladly sign your enclosed mandate.

The humorous missive struck a chord with those on the receiving end and they persuaded their boss to extend the cheque payment facility beyond the three-month grace period. In Britain, when you want to make a point, it is best done with a light touch.

British managers too tend to have a negative view of conflict. That assertion might be greeted with scepticism by foreigners who are familiar with Britain's adversarial style of industrial relations. But the whole point about industrial confrontations is that they are depersonalized. The conflict is transferred to a third party.

Setting labour relations aside, there is, in the British view, something rather ungentlemanly about open conflict between managers. Even the ultimate show-down, redundancy, is generally a low-key affair, couched in euphemism. With much clearing of throats and visible reluctance, bosses will talk of having to 'let someone go', evoking the image of an individual desperately straining at the leash, when the opposite is generally the case. Worse still, managerial unwillingness to grasp this nettle often leads to another euphemism, 'constructive dismissal', whereby the unwanted are gradually stripped of responsibility and forced out through isolation and loss of self-esteem.

AGAINST THE GRAIN

"Don't tell me – you finally fired him!"

British managers are reluctant to 'blow their lids'. It shows a lack of control. Something like the understated verdict of one regional director that 'This report doesn't make very happy reading' is generally enough to get the message across. Another director had a habit of expressing his displeasure at bad news by claiming that it had given him the 'screaming heebie-jeebies' – thereby focusing on the impact of the news rather than on the person responsible for it.

Conflict, in British management, is not seen as essentially creative, as a means of correcting deviations, testing ideas or of proving oneself. In America, and Germany to some extent, forthrightness is seen as desirable. By British standards, German managers are more outspoken, more critical upwards and more ready to indulge in the censure of others. There is no phrase in German for 'don't rock the boat' and they rock it all the time.

In Britain, refusals will be softened. There is a reticence to pronounce an outright 'no'. British managers are more likely to respond: 'I'm afraid I would have difficulty doing that just now.' Even mundane requests will be ushered in by, 'Is there any chance of . . .?'; and something like, 'I really would rather . . .' amounts to insistence. It is a convention, in Britain, that instructions be disguised as polite invitations.

This lack of candour in British management was noted by a senior American executive working in a British subsidiary:

> One of the things I've found in our organisation here is a reluctance on the part of an Englishman to debate with his superior. Americans have to understand when working with English people that very often an Englishman will be silent when he doesn't agree with you. Communication may be non-verbal. Americans rely a great deal on language, and they tend more to spontaneous combustion in their management style.
>
> (*Director,* April 1988, p.46)

Of course, the managerial function requires managers to tell others what to do, and this can lead to resistance and resentment. In a culture where restraint is the norm, humour serves as a veil for embarrassment and aggression. Sir Brian Wolfson explained:

> Humour is our way of saying the things that the Japanese would say by getting drunk — and then whatever's been said doesn't count the next morning. You can, with humour, be far more acerbic than you can without it.

Humour allows British managers to be tough and to point out behavioural irregularities without losing either dignity or compassion. As Sir John Harvey-Jones confirmed:

> Much of what we say in Britain is indirect. We tend to be evasive. But sometimes you have to call a spade a bloody shovel — and the only way to do that without offence is to use humour.

So British managers tend to shun the confrontational approach to management. But nor do they take the overtly consensual route favoured by, say, the Swedes. British managers are concerned to avoid disharmony among the group or disloyalty to the boss, and that will override all but the most fundamental disagreement. But if they seek neither to command nor consult, how do they ever get things done through other people? The answer is that British managers tend to favour a persuasive mode.

Part of the reason that Britons frame their commands to sound like requests is that the persuasion mode requires the *perception* of choice. When someone is asked, 'Would you mind . . .', 'I wonder if . . .', refusal is *de facto* difficult, but remains possible. A semblance of choice is essential for there to be a favour. Deprived of choice, the receiver is merely carrying out an instruction. Thus 'Would you mind . . .' is a million miles away from 'I'm sure you don't mind . . .'.

Similarly, decisions that may, in truth, be unilateral decisions are sold with diplomacy and a heavy dose of that organizational cure-all, humour: 'I've got some good news for you – if you like hard work.' Or take the example of the operations director who, needing to take the edge off an instruction, announced, 'My wife sorted out that problem last night, so that is how we are going to do it . . .'

British managers want to get their own way, but they want to cajole people into acceptance. There is a premium on the ability to convince or gently manipulate others. In the words of one brewery departmental manager:

> I pride myself on knowing all 52 people on the shop-floor – and at least five out of their ten foibles. I know who supports West Ham, who does *The Times* crossword, and who's mad as a hatter. I would generally work on those, especially if I thought there might be some difficulty in pushing something through.

British managers, then, do not go in for unbridled displays of naked power. As one marketing manager saw it, 'I would never use the "pips on the shoulder". That's a virility test and the manager who needs that is in the wrong job.' So, it is all right for British managers to have rank, but to 'pull it' is a measure of last resort – a cop-out, an admission of failure.

Nor do they want to get involved in protracted discussions before the event. They prefer to chivvy along rather than ordain or negotiate, though with deferential undercurrents. This means, among other things, that they go about persuading superiors in a different way from persuading subordinates. Humour is a particularly versatile tool when it comes to hitting the right persuasive note. Indeed, humour could be considered the mainstay of the persuasion mode.

The trick, as British managers see it, is to find solutions that people will accept. Getting your own way is primarily a matter of having a clear idea of what's in it for the other party, and slanting the approach accordingly. Take, for example, the quality control manager who wanted to persuade his colleague to produce a process map for his quality project by a certain deadline. Instead of trying to appeal to his professional pride or the needs of the business, he bet him a pint that he would not be able to complete it in time. The challenge was taken up and fulfilled, demonstrating that getting things done in Britain is about exercising subtle social pressure.

Clearly, in Britain, much is achieved by means of social acceptance, offering or withholding it. Besides persuasion in the conventional sense of reasoned and reasonable argument, persuasion British-style is also about things like threats veiled as humour. A remark such as 'people have been shot for less' can give a clear indication of displeasure. The rules may not be spelled out, but there is a strong sense of when people are 'overstepping the mark'. The hint of ostracism can be a powerful weapon.

British managers set much store by the idea of rejection from and admission to groups. Ensuring that juniors do what is expected of them is often about holding out the possibility of 'joining the club'; compliance is a question of establishing a personal relationship whereby the junior in question 'won't let the side down.'

In British companies, then, getting other people to do things is a matter of putting your personality and sense of humour on the line. In America, France or Germany, on the other hand, doing what the boss says is not a personal 'favour' but rather an act of faith in his or her judgement. In many ways, persuasion is to amateurism what authority is to professionalism.

Laughing
8 Matters

In a way, humour makes business grow up, which is important. It gives business a sense of place — it helps business realize it's not the most important thing in the world.

(Sir Peter Parker, former chairman, British Rail)

As far back as the Hawthorne Studies half a century ago, Elton Mayo and his team identified joking and horseplay as significant features of the informal social processes in the workplace. Humour, if only because it is accompanied by smiling and laughter, must be the most obvious aspect of interpersonal relations. Yet the role of humour in the managerial process remains virtually unrecorded. Why so?

IN A MANNER OF SPEAKING

The neglect of humour in management literature is actually part of a wider disregard for the broken play – as opposed to the set pieces – of management work.

Airport bookshops are awash with paperbacks on speech-making, handling meetings or negotiations, and report-writing. Quite rightly, for these are show-case opportunities in which managers are highly exposed, and their credibility is held up to public scrutiny. Poor performance in these situations can wipe out years of good work behind the scenes.

The fact remains that such occasions are pretty scarce for most managers. They spend the bulk of their time talking to people informally, in unstructured situations. Yet very little attention is paid to how managers inform, inspire or elicit co-operation on a daily basis – which is normally of far greater importance to organizations in realizing their purpose.

To get things done through other people, managers select a range of modes of speech which go from the exact to the ambiguous; from the stark to the poetic. At one extreme they may discuss the computing needs of the department, and at the other, they will deliver something akin to Henry V's team talk before Agincourt.

Certain modes of speech, humour being one, are better suited to imparting particular types of message to different audiences. A manager who wishes to clarify or to convey an impression of certainty will tend to use plain speaking or precise jargon, as epitomized by the use of accounting terminology. Managers talk easily of 'the bottom line' whether they are addressing financial issues or not. Objects, acts and events are reduced to the common denominator of money. Even people may be 'written off' or labelled 'a liability'.

Managers wishing to arouse emotion, enthusiasm and commitment may employ rhetoric. Symbols and metaphors will be invoked to create shared visions. For instance, managers plunder the familiar vocabulary of sport – 'hitting the opposition for six', 'keeping your eye on the ball' – for the purposes of motivation. They seek out analogies and invent slogans which will inspire and invigorate their troops. As Sir Brian Wolfson put it, 'I think what the skilful manager does is to choose images which paint pictures in people's minds. You look for trigger words that switch people on.'

Another way of making an impact on people is to use the language of the gutter. Against the pristine backdrop of organizational restraint, swearing can have a blistering effect. It is a way of bringing people up sharp, of shaking up complacency, of indicating determination or reiterating a particular set of priorities. Of course, for maximum impact expletives have to be used sparingly. Swearing should not be abused.

The same could be said for the use of humorous invective. The *leitmotiv* of this book has been that, used selectively, humour can be a key managerial tool in difficult situations. Much can be achieved through humour which could not be achieved, as fast or as painlessly, by other means. As Sir Brian Wolfson explains:

Overall, humour is a way of changing atmosphere. That's the umbrella which covers all proactive attempts at humour. The appropriate use of humour can defuse, amuse, motivate, challenge and completely change the atmosphere. It's one of the least understood and most valid tools of management.

An awareness of how language is used, both by managers and on them, is important. Where a leap of faith or imagination is required, rhetoric, humour or even flattery are more likely to do the trick than plain speaking. The injection of humour or an expletive brings an element of suprise into a situation.

Managers have to marshall their linguistic resources, to mix and match for effect. For instance, the use of rhetoric and plain speaking in tandem allows managers to arouse and direct behaviour, thereby mobilizing individuals. The idea is to gear the type of speech to the audience, the message and the desired effect. But where is the research? Unplanned oral communication receives short shrift in the management literature.

Partly, then, the absence of research on humour in management is merely a consequence of the lack of attention paid to how managers actually do their jobs – and their predilection for spoken, informal interaction.

But there are additional complications, for academics and practitioners alike, regarding the legitimization of humour in management.

MIRTH CONTROL

For academics, the intentional use of humour by managers is not easy to record. The moment that it is subjected to scrutiny it has a habit of disappearing. Just try telling managers you have come to observe them putting humour to work, and watch it dry up. Nor can genuine and spontaneous mirth be reproduced under controlled conditions. The elusiveness of humour and its resistance to orthodox research methods has inhibited researchers. One way round this obstacle is simply not to let on that humour is the focus of interest and to use the cover of a mainstream research topic, such as leadership style.

Not only is humour tricky to observe, but it is fragile. Taken out of context and analysed, it invariably loses its edge. Wordsworth's warning that 'we murder to dissect' is nowhere truer than with humour. Even if the humorous sound-bite does survive the transition from the oral to the written medium, it is unlikely to be relevant to other managers in other situations. As humour consultant Malcolm Kushner points out, 'It depends on who orginates the humor and at whom it's directed, as well as where and when it is uttered. These considerations defy the formulation of simple rules' (Kushner, 1990, p.188).

The fact that humour is situation-specific sits uneasily with the view of management that we have imported from America. Management is touted as a science, with an acquirable set of skills and a body of knowledge which can be classified and passed on. Humour is a faculty, not a set of principles that can be taught. It feeds, not on a store of jokes, but on a view of the world. It arises out of the situations one finds oneself in. As Sir Brian Wolfson confirmed; 'It's to do with keeping one's tongue in cheek in certain circumstances, rather than joke-telling.'

Sanctioning humour as a legitimate management tool would therefore go against everything that management, the discipline, has tried to establish for itself over the last century. Even the management bestsellers of the past fifteen years which proclaimed their faith in the human side of business and the charisma of leaders have not dared to grasp the humour nettle. This capacity of management authors to ignore 'the bleeding obvious' partly explains why practitioners have little faith in 'learned' books.

Whilst academics and consultants have problems in reconciling humour and management, one would expect retiring chief executives to use their biographies to set the record straight. But for them too, joke seems to be a four-letter word. Perhaps for fear of appearing foolish or of jeopardizing future directorships, they keep quiet. Even forthright Sir John Harvey-Jones, whose humour is an integral part of his management style, devotes no more than five lines to laughter in his *Reflections on Leadership* (1988). The upshot of this is that humour remains the manager's best kept secret.

The official line, then, is that humour has no part in an environment governed by rationality and professionalism. Time-and-motion studies have prescribed times for everything from sitting on chairs to applying rubber bands, but there is no time for laugther. Managerial minds are expected to concentrate on the task in hand, and the intrusion of humour is deemed to distract from that focus.

Take the example of GrandMet's Sir Allen Sheppard. He is renowned for his readiness to see the funny side of things. But, on occasion, this has worked against him and the company. One respondent in a MORI research poll spontaneously cited the chairman's sense of humour as a weakness of the company. As Sheppard himself saw it:

> There is a feeling in some parts of the City that we're not really serious about what we're doing. They think we should be desperately worried, particularly given the radical reshaping of the business in the last few years. There's a general feeling that if I'm not near to a state of mental collapse, I can't be taking it seriously.

Actually, the belief that humour automatically shuts out seriousness is fundamentally flawed. Sheppard went on to shoot down this fallacy:

> The problem is that people get confused between humour and lack of seriousness. Take our annual general meeting. It's a very serious occasion. The shareholders own the company and you have to take whatever questions they ask absolutely seriously in terms of giving proper professional answers. On the other hand, you don't have to run the meeting as though it were the gateway into Belsen.

Levity and seriousness, then, are not mutually exclusive. It is possible to joke about the most serious matters – death, politics, religion, not to mention profit – without detracting from their importance. What is not possible is to joke and, at the same time, remain austere.

Another point of confusion is the failure to distinguish between taking one's work (jobs, problems, challenges) seriously and taking oneself seriously. Realistic, professional and committed need not mean dour, uptight and remote. Sir Peter Parker lays this myth to rest:

> There are times when you get so wrapped up in your work, that you forget what on earth you're trying to do. I have yet to find anything worth achieving which you can't have a good time doing.

The need for a certain detachment between oneself and one's work is vital. It affords a measure of protection for the individual from the pernicious influence of any organization.

AIN'T NO SANITY CLAUSE

Organizations and professions generate a kind of collective insanity. They cultivate particular ways of doing things, of dressing and behaving. The world they create is not just abnormal, but insidiously so. Even individuals determined not to get involved inexorably get sucked into the petty status-mongering, the infighting, and become bewitched by the jargon and rituals.

Miles Kington relates the pitiful case of Roger, an apparently successful executive of 35, with an incurable disability:

> He has a speech problem. One which prevents him from speaking intelligently in the presence of his business peers. Here is something Roger said recently to a colleague: 'The client has overly high expectations, market penetration-wise.'
>
> What does it mean? Nothing, I'm afraid. Roger is talking nonsense. But did his colleague turn round and say: 'What is that meant to mean, for heaven's sake?' No, I'm afraid he did not. What he said was: 'Well, when you're in a customer-focused situation, you need more product awareness than their sort of low-profile image is going to generate.'
>
> Yes, when Roger talks nonsense, his colleague talks nonsense back to him.
>
> (*Independent*, 13 April 1992, p.18)

Business people are not alone in suffering from this complaint. Self-contained communities everywhere cultivate their own ways of talking and behaving.

Working in any organization, then, requires a sort of willed self-hypnosis. It is a bit like playing a sport. In order to move forward, it is necessary to pretend, and temporarily believe, that it matters a great deal. Suspension of disbelief takes many forms. Managers learn to simulate passion and disappointment for monthly sales figures, they experience elation at clinching a deal, they quake at the thought of being summoned to the boss's office. They grow to

like colleagues whose only redeeming qualities are their forthrightness and consistency, and they have nothing but contempt for
kindly ditherers. They sell customers products which they do not
need in order to meet their quotas. In advanced cases, executives
may be more bothered about walking into the managing director's
office sporting a rogue nasal hair than with the enforced
redundancy of long-standing colleagues.

This loss of empathy and decency is encouraged by organizations. They make themselves central to people's lives by holding out
promises. They promise intrinsic and extrinsic rewards. Along with
the money and security, the power and influence, there is the
seduction of recognition, approval and a sense of belonging –
acceptance as part of the 'big happy family'. But membership hinges
on adhering to corporate norms, often at the expense of personal
views or beliefs. A certain numbness develops. Rather than
acknowledge their feelings, individuals prefer to look forward to
the weekend, to holidays or to retirement.

THE WAY WE DO THINGS AROUND HERE

*"Next, I want you to roll from the fax machine to the copier, demonstrating
proper control of your vehicle."*

In this sometimes warped environment with its topsy-turvy
values, humour is a vital counter-force. It has a civilizing influence,
both interpersonally and in terms of exposing organizational
excesses. Corporate absurdity is revealed in all its glory when taken
out of context. Humour is easily derived from transposing

workplace practices into alternative settings, or translating business euphemisms into everyday language: ' "Empowering subordinates", he calls it. Dumping all his crap on us, more like.'

Humour provides momentary respite from oppressive norms. It allows managers to disentangle their identity from their work roles, to defend their own psychic territory, and to look beyond life within the organization. The poignant testimony of one distribution manager is a salutary reminder that, however compelling the corporate drama, it is only a drama:

> One of my daughters had to have an abortion. Another one got married without inviting me to the wedding, and the wimp she married has gone off and left her with three children. At times you want to cut your throat. So when you're talking about problems, what's a problem? Compared to that, the problems at work are light relief.

Humour allows organizational troubles to be reduced to the proportions of a child's disturbances. We are effectively saying to ourselves: 'Look here! This is all this seemingly dangerous world amounts to.' Humour lifts us out the myopic, anxious, inflexible mode we find ourselves in most of the time, and enables us to take the broad view, to think more intelligently. As Sir Peter Parker sees it:

> We delude ourselves into thinking that the world is all about us, so it takes us by surprise when reality throws a spanner in the works. So many things are beyond us for the simple reason that we're looking at our front wheels and pedalling like hell the whole time.

Humour helps managers to regain their sense of perspective. That is not just essential for their personal survival. The survival of the organization also depends on keeping a grip on reality.

JUST A DELUSION

Story-telling is a basic human instinct, a means of organizing the mess and the chaos we experience into recognizable patterns. Thus, retrospective accounts of corporate strategies exude a reassuring blend of certainty and coherence. Their whole tenor is one of easy control and total premeditation. Triumphant coups are presented as the natural culmination of careful planning and purposeful implementation. This, of course, is misleading. Rational descriptions are usually afterthoughts used to cloak all the emotions and intuitions that were actually involved in an aura of sober business judgement. Humour serves to redress the balance. It helps to restore some of the windfalls and flukes that were selectively erased by the distorting lens of hindsight.

The processes of fabrication and simplification which produce corporate myths and folklore require relatively little work to sustain them. But to challenge these myths sometimes requires considerable insight and courage. Humour allows us to see the truth behind the inspired vision and to deflate pretentious claims. Humour, then, does not debase business, it merely reminds us that business is already debased. One need only look at the pomp and circumstance surrounding certain business presentations for confirmation. As Sir Peter Parker observes:

> You see these AGMs; people standing there with shadowed lights, and they open their mouths and a visual display appears, and they turn round and read it to you. I find a degree of abnormality, and pomposity and self-righteousness about the way business presents itself. And that *amour propre* can be pricked with humour.

THE BLAND LEADING THE BLAND

"He's miming to a tape from head office."

Humour teaches us to see organizations as they really are, undulled by corporate myth. Businesses have an endless capacity for self-delusion, often heightened by success. It is in this make-believe world that the seeds of complacency and eventual downfall germinate. Humour is therefore a vital force in the direction of critical reappraisal and renewal. It challenges that which is taken for granted and draws attention to the mismatch between hype and reality. It is a vital cure for corporate flatulence.

Humour helps the organization keep in touch with reality in another way too, by facilitating the upward flow of information. In most companies, the channels of communication are geared towards flushing information down through the organization rather than sucking up information from below. Humour provides one of the few channels for rectifying that bias.

The normal rules are momentarily suspended when humour is invoked. Individuals are briefly relieved of responsibility for their words or actions. They are free to parody the organization and to question its conventions without anyone taking offence or having to fake indignation. This is especially important for those near the base of the organization who may use humour to communicate criticism, fears or ideas, thereby confirming the principle that light things float to the top.

In an environment which is not always conducive to the free flow of information, humour provides an alternative channel of communication – a means of overcoming organizational gravity, in every sense.

THE LAST LAUGH

It transpires that, far from sabotaging organizational purpose, humour is instrumental in pursuing it. The business environment is a consummate generator of paradox and inconsistency, and humour thrives on these. It could even be said that humour exists in order to compensate for the inability of our rational view of the world to accommodate disorder.

The presence of humour in business serves as a constant reminder of our limited understanding of organizational processes and human behaviour. It is from the disparity between our expectations and reality that humour springs. In every plan gone wrong, in every platitude rendered paradoxical, in every principle disproved, in every fact caught in duplicity, there is comic energy waiting to be unleashed. What were once worrying contradictions or inconsistencies become intriguing toys, to be played with and enjoyed. Jeremy Bullmore explains:

Humour is that which most efficiently recognizes that we are living in an imperfect world, with imperfect arguments and that things are insane, illogical, and irrational. And the only way we can live with that fact is to laugh.

Thus, while it is true that humour mocks existing organizational patterns and activities, that is the price to be paid for preserving them. For instance, humour exposes corporate myths and, if the discrepancy between pretence and reality is sufficiently marked, may even contribute to their undoing. But for the most part, humour allows the qualified myth to live on and fulfil its inspirational function.

Humour also helps to sustain managerial effort. Occupying the lulls between the rhythms of work, humour makes the process of work, as well as its output, more satisfying and meaningful. Humour energizes and unites those who partake of it. It facilitates the co-ordination of effort and makes organizational pressures more bearable. It is the safety-valve that makes collective endeavours possible. For all these reasons humour is an organizational necessity, not a luxury.

More surprisingly perhaps, the usage of humour and the practice of management turn out to be closely related. Both require that vital, yet intangible faculty, judgement. Hitting the right humorous chord demands sensitivity to other people, to their frame of mind and motivation, and to the image that one is projecting. Managers must be in touch with the prevailing mood. They also need a sense of timing. Managers have to find the right moment to say or do something.

The effective use of humour therefore demands interpersonal sensitivity as well as comic insight. That is why people who are 'relentlessly funny' are such wearing colleagues: they have the insight but lack the accompanying sensitivity. As Jeremy Bullmore sees it, 'If your style of humour is not appreciated by the rest of the team, then it's not humour. It may be funny to you, but if no one else laughs, then it's not funny.'

The idea is not to bludgeon people's funny bones but rather to empathize with their circumstances. Humour is not a cure-all and it is not always appropriate. As one production manager put it, 'I feel you should use humour like a lamp-post – for illumination, not to lean on.'

DISCRETION IS THE BETTER PART OF HUMOUR

"Do you like my new executive toy, Simpkins?"

Humour, then, is but one skill, albeit a valuable one, in the manager's repertoire. Knowing when and how to use humour is just another facet of the manager's craft. Sir John Harvey-Jones spells it out in his own inimitable style:

> The manager has to be extremely sensitive — I know this, of course, makes people fall about — but actually management is a very sensitive job. You need to be master of every single club in the golf bag, but the art is to continually choose the appropriate club for the particular day in the particular situation.
>
> (*Take It from the Top*, Video Arts, 1990)

Managers who see no need to make any concession to humour are unlikely to fail, but they may find themselves hacking their way to the green with a putter.

Beyond helping managers to get the job done and organizations to function, humour also has intrinsic value. Humour takes us out of ourselves, it enables us to reflect, it brings us closer together and makes us more humane. The joke is on us, for humour is in fact no laughing matter.

Once upon a time we believed that intuition was incompatible with management. Today, we labour under a similar misapprehension by excluding humour from the official portrayal of management work. Yet humour is the sharpest arrow in the manager's quiver. It is time that this fact was acknowledged – for until managers are presented with a better picture of what their work involves and how they go about it, how can they consciously improve?

Bibliography

Augustine, Norman R., *Augustine's Laws* (New York: Viking Penguin, 1986).

Barsoux, Jean-Louis, Is business a laughing matter? *Director*, June 1991, 65–8.

Braham, James, Lighten up. *Industry Week*, 7 March 1988, 49–52.

Bryce, Lee, *The Influential Woman* (London: Arrow Books, 1989).

Bullmore, Jeremy, *Behind the Scenes in Advertising* (Henley-on-Thames: NTC Publications, 1991).

Business Week, Oops: Who's excellent now? 5 November 1984, 46–55.

Casson, John, *Using Words* (London: Duckworth, 1968).

Chapman, Antony J. and Foot, Hugh C., *Humour and Laughter: Theory, Research and Applications* (London: John Wiley & Sons, 1976).

Cockburn, Claud, *Cockburn Sums Up* (London: Quartet Books, 1981).

Cooper, Anthony A., *Sensus Communis: An Essay on the Freedom of Wit and Humour*, 1709 (cited in *The Oxford Dictionary of Quotations*, 2nd edn, Oxford: Oxford University Press, 1977).

Coyne, Harold, *Scam: How Con Men Use the Phone to Steal Your Money* (London: Duckworth, 1991).

Dahrendorf, Ralf, *On Britain* (London: British Broadcasting Corporation, 1982).

Dalton, Melvin, *Men Who Manage* (New York: Wiley, 1959).

Davis, William, *The Corporate Infighter's Handbook* (London: Sidgwick & Jackson, 1984).

de Bono, Edward, *Lateral Thinking for Management* (Harmonds-worth: Penguin Books, 1971).

Decker, Wayne, H., Style, gender, and humor effects in evaluating leaders. *Mid-Atlantic Journal of Business*, **27** (2), June 1991, 117–28.

Drucker, Peter, *The Practice of Management* (London: Pan Piper, 1955).

Duncan, W. Jack and Feisal, J. Philip, No laughing matter: Patterns of humor in the workplace. *Organizational Dynamics*, **17**, Spring 1989, 18–30.

Duncan, W. Jack, Smeltzer, Larry R. and Leap, Terry, Humor and work: Applications of joking behavior to management. *Journal of Management*, 1990, **16** (2), 255–78.

Enright, Dennis J., *The Alluring Problem* (Oxford: OUP, 1986).

Ewart, Gavin, *Pleasures of the Flesh* (Oxford: OUP, 1966).

Fletcher, Winston, *The Ad Makers* (London: Michael Joseph, 1973).

Fletcher, Winston, *Commercial Breaks* (London: Advertising Press, 1984).

Fletcher, Winston, *Meetings, Meetings* (Sevenoaks: Hodder & Stoughton, 1985).

Freud, Sigmund, *Jokes and Their Relation to the Unconscious* (Harmondsworth: Penguin Books, 1981).

Goldstein, Jeffrey H. and McGhee, Paul E. (eds), *The Psychology of Humour* (London: Academic Press, 1972).

Gruner, Charles R., *Understanding Laughter* (Chicago: Nelson-Hall, 1978).

Gurewitch, Morton, *Comedy: the Irrational Vision* (New York: Cornell University Press, 1975).

Hartley, Robert F., *Management Mistakes* (New York: John Wiley & Sons, 1986).

Harvey-Jones, John, *Making It Happen: Reflections on Leadership* (London: Collins, 1988).

Hearn, Jeff and Parkin, Wendy, *'Sex' at 'Work': The Power and Paradox of Organisational Sexuality* (Brighton: Wheatsheaf, 1987).

Heller, Robert, *The Making of Managers* (London: Penguin, 1989).

Hobbes, Thomas, *On Human Nature*, 1650 (cited in *The Oxford Dictionary of Quotations*, 2nd edn, Oxford: Oxford University Press, 1977).

Jay, Anthony, *Management and Machiavelli* (Sevenoaks: Hodder & Stoughton, 1967).

Kennedy, Carol, Where British managers have the edge. *Director*, June 1988, 125–7.

Kharbanda, Om Prakash and Stallworthy, Ernest A., *Management Disasters* (Aldershot: Gower, 1986).

Kimmins, C. W., *The Springs of Laughter* (London: Methuen, 1928).

Kington, Miles, *Moreover* (London: Robson Books, 1982).

Koenig, Fedrick, *Rumor in the Marketplace* (Massachusetts: Auburn House, 1985).

Koestler, Arthur, *The Act of Creation* (London: Hutchinson, 1964).

Kotter, John, P., *The General Managers* (New York: The Free Press, 1982).

Kraft, Eric, *Herb 'n' Lorna* (Sevenoaks: Hodder & Stoughton, 1989).

Kushner, Malcolm, *The Light Touch: How to Use Humor for Business Success* (New York: Simon & Schuster, 1990).

Lawrence, Peter, *Invitation to Management* (Oxford: Blackwell, 1986).

Lewis, Jeremy (ed.), *The Chatto Book of Office Life* (London: Chatto & Windus, 1992).

Lockyer, Keith and Jones, Steven, The function factor. *Management Today*, September 1980, 53-64.

Lodge, David, *Nice Work* (Harmondsworth: Penguin, 1989).

McGhee, Paul E., *Humor: Its Origin and Development* (San Francisco: W. H. Freeman & Company, 1979).

McGhee, Paul E. and Goldstein, Jeffrey H., *Handbook of Humour Research*, Vols 1 and 2 (New York: Springer-Verlag, 1983).

Malone, Paul B., Humour: a double-edged tool for today's managers. *Academy of Management Review*, 1980, **5** (3), 357–60.

Mant, Alistair, *The Rise and Fall of the British Manager* (Basingstoke: Macmillan, 1977).

Martin, Thomas L., *Malice in Blunderland* (New York: McGraw-Hill, 1973).

Meredith, George and Bergson, Henri, *Comedy* (Baltimore: John Hopkins University Press, 1980).

Metcalf, C. W. and Felible, Roma, *Lighten Up: Survival Skills for People under Pressure* (Reading, MA: Addison-Wesley, 1992).

Mikes, George, *How to Be an Alien* (London: André Deutsch, 1946).

Mikes, George, *The Land of the Rising Yen* (London: André Deutsch, 1970).

Miles, Ros, *Danger! Men at Work* (London: Macdonald, 1983).

Miles, Ros, Sex on the job, *Cosmopolitan*, July 1985, 110–14.

Mintzberg, Henry, *The Nature of Managerial Work* (New York: Harper & Row, 1973).

Mole, John, *Mind Your Manners* (London: The Industrial Society, 1990).

Monbiot, Raymond, *How to Manage Your Boss* (Newbury: Scope Books, 1980).

Morgan, Gareth, *Creative Organization Theory* (California: Sage, 1989).

Muir, Frank, *The Oxford Book of Humorous Prose* (Oxford: OUP, 1990).

Mulkay, Michael, *On Humour* (Cambridge: Polity Press, 1988).

Nash, Walter, *The Language of Humour* (London: Longman, 1985).

Nulty, Peter, America's toughest bosses. *Fortune*, 27 February 1989, 24–30.

Packard, Vince, *The Hidden Persuaders* (Harmondsworth: Penguin, 1960).

Parkinson, C. Northcote, *Parkinson's Law* (London: John Murray, 1958).

Peter, Laurence and Hull, Raymond, *The Peter Principle: Why Things Go Wrong* (New York: William Morrow & Company, 1969).

Peters, Thomas and Waterman, Robert, *In Search of Excellence: Lessons from America's Best-run Companies* (New York: Harper & Row, 1982).

Pile, Stephen, *The Book of Heroic Failures* (London: Futura, 1980).

Powell, Chris and Paton, George E.C. (eds), *Humour in Society* (Basingstoke: Macmillan, 1988).

Reynolds, Larry, Laughter is the best motivator. *Management Review*, July 1989, **78**, (7), 58–9.

Rosenblum, Gene, *Is Your Car a Sex Symbol?* (New York: Hawthorn, 1972).

Scase, Richard and Goffee, Robert, Women in management: towards a research agenda. *International Journal of Human Resource Management*, June 1990, **1** (1), 107–25.

Schaeffer, Neil, *The Art of Laughter* (New York: Columbia University Press, 1981).

Schnaars, Steven P., *Megamistakes* (New York: The Free Press, 1989).

Simcock, Corinne, *A Head for Business* (London: Kogan Page, 1992).

Smith, Denis M., *Mussolini* (London: Weidenfeld & Nicolson, 1982).

Smith, Paul, *The Complete Book of Office Mis-Practice* (London: Routledge & Kegan Paul, 1984).

Stewart, Rosemary, *Managing Today and Tomorrow* (Basingstoke: Macmillan, 1991).

Townsend, Robert, *Up the Organisation* (London: Michael Joseph, 1970).

Trump, Donald, *The Art of the Deal* (London: Century, 1988).

Trump, Donald, *Surviving at the Top* (New York: Random House, 1990).

Valeriani, Richard, *Travels with Henry* (Boston: Houghton Mifflin, 1979).

Weinberger, Marc G. and Spotts, Harlan E., Humor in US versus UK TV commercials: A comparison. *Journal of Advertising*, 1989, **18** (2), 39–44.

Willeford, William, *The Fool and His Scepter* (London: Edward Arnold, 1969).

Wilson, Christopher P., *Jokes: Form, Content, Use and Function* (London: Academic Press, 1979).

Zeldin, Theodore, *The French* (London: Collins, 1980).

Index